T0153158

LET'S ALL PLAY

Other Redleaf Press Books by Jeff A. Johnson and Denita Dinger

Let's Play:
(Un)Curriculum Early Learning Adventures

Let Them Play:
An Early Learning (Un)Curriculum

LET'S ALL PLAY

A Group Learning

(Un)Curriculum

Jeff A. Johnson and Denita Dinger

 Redleaf Press®
www.redleafpress.org
800-423-8309

Published by Redleaf Press
10 Yorkton Court
St. Paul, MN 55117
www.redleafpress.org

© 2015 by Jeff A. Johnson and Denita Dinger

All rights reserved. Unless otherwise noted on a specific page, no portion of this publication may be reproduced or transmitted in any form or by any means, electronic or mechanical, including photocopying, recording, or capturing on any information storage and retrieval system, without permission in writing from the publisher, except by a reviewer, who may quote brief passages in a critical article or review to be printed in a magazine or newspaper, or electronically transmitted on radio, television, or the Internet.

First edition 2015
Cover design by Jim Handrigan
Cover photograph by STEFANOLUNARDI/iStock/ThinkStock
Interior design by Ryan Scheife, Mayfly Design
Typeset in the Alberta MT and Myriad Pro typefaces
Printed in the United States of America

21 20 19 18 17 16 15 14   1 2 3 4 5 6 7 8

Library of Congress Cataloging-in-Publication Data

Johnson, Jeff A., 1969-
  Let's all play : a group-learning (un)curriculum / Jeff A. Johnson,
Denita Dinger.
       pages cm
  Summary: "Let's All Play provides all-new adventures that support
children's social skill development through thoughtful group play,
interaction, and conversation. This book also encourages you to reflect
on the value of children's play through deep thinking activities"—
Provided by publisher.
  ISBN 978-1-60554-364-2 (paperback)
1. Play—United States. 2. Early childhood education—United States.
3. Early childhood education—Curricula—United States. I. Dinger,
Denita. II. Title.
  LB1139.35.P55J65 2015
  790.0973—dc23
                        2014019838

Printed on acid-free paper

To mistakes, failures, patience, and tenacity,
for without them I would have missed so many opportunities

—Denita

To Tasha, my *One True Love* and favorite playmate

—Jeff

The human brain is an apparatus, first and foremost, for dealing with the social environment.

—Judith Rich Harris, *The Nurture Assumption:*
Why Children Turn Out the Way They Do

Abundant research exists on the importance of *social skills* for success in school. "Whole" children attend school; they don't just send their brains along. Nurturing children's social and emotional skills in preschool enables them to profit from school instruction. Children who thrive in preschool are prepared to become members of a classroom community where the individual's needs come after the needs of the group—a tough lesson for young children. Children who do well in preschool listen to directions, pay attention, solve disputes with words, and focus on tasks without constant supervision. Recent research suggests that they learn these skills through playful activities.

—Kathy Hirsh-Pasek, Roberta Michnick Golinkoff, Laura E. Berk,
and Dorothy G. Singer, *A Mandate for Playful Learning in Preschool:*
Presenting the Evidence

Contents

Acknowledgments

Thanks to photographer Leslie Dionne (you're a FWP, Leslie!), Sachelle Fidler, and the rest of the gang at Little Munchkins Preschool Center for their help with photos. Thanks to Brittney Mendiola and Cheryl Mendiola at Tuggy's Tots Preschool for the photos they provided. Thanks to Lori Atchison of Lori Atchison Photography (www.latchphoto.com) for the photos she provided. Thanks to the gang at Redleaf Press for letting us do another book together. Thanks to all the folks who've supported our previous efforts and helped with this project.

Thank you to my dad for encouraging me to chase my dreams and for teaching me the importance of optimism, relationships, and a full tank. —Denita

Thanks to Tasha, Starbucks, and rum. —Jeff

Introduction: Social Play

We humans are social creatures. We are driven to connect and interact with each other. Our brains need social contact.

Social skills are skills we will use throughout the entirety of our lives, yet in many early learning settings, play—the primary way young children practice and hone skills—is disappearing and being replaced with an unrelenting rush to early academics in preparation for school and the high-pressure, high-stakes testing that drives it.

Social skills are vital because they help kids prepare not only for all the human-to-human interactions to come in their lives but also for school.

- -

Importantly, not only do cognitive and social skills reinforce one another, but social skills can actually *lead* to better cognitive skills, especially for children with average cognitive abilities. Children with advanced social skills may be better at getting additional information from teachers, understanding others' points of view, cooperating with teachers and peers, and displaying initiative in the classroom. A large body of research documenting the predictive value of preschool children's social maturity for later school success indicates that school readiness should not be assessed just in terms of cognitive attainments but also in terms of social attainments that forecast children's adjustment to formal schooling.

**—Kathy Hirsh-Pasek, Roberta Michnick Golinkoff,
Laura E. Berk, and Dorothy G. Singer,** *A Mandate for
Playful Learning in Preschool: Presenting the Evidence*

- -

Ask a few kindergarten teachers: most likely, they'll say they are more concerned with social skills than academic skills.

When kindergarten teachers are surveyed about their students, they say that the biggest problem they face is not children who don't know their letters and numbers; it is kids who don't know how to manage their tempers or calm themselves down after a provocation.

—Paul Tough, *How Children Succeed: Grit, Curiosity, and the Hidden Power of Character*

This book is about playful ways to support children while they develop and practice social skills. It is a follow-up to our 2012 book, *Let Them Play: An Early Learning (Un)Curriculum*, and our 2013 book, *Let's Play: (Un)Curriculum Early Learning Adventures*, and is intended for early learning professionals and families who want to support hands-on, child-led, play-based learning. It helps adults accustomed to rigidly structured, adult-led early learning curriculum ease into an (un)curriculum that supports good old-fashioned play and trusts kids as learners. Easing into an (un)curriculum is important, because for many people, the idea of giving up control and letting children lead is very scary.

Think of the following information as the book's FAQ page. If an (un)curriculum is new to you, the FAQs will bring you up to speed.

What is an (un)curriculum?

An (un)curriculum is hands-on, child-led, play-based learning supported by the preparation, encouragement, and facilitation of an adult. Here are the principles of an (un)curriculum:

- An (un)curriculum is supported by brain-development research.

- An (un)curriculum nurtures the individual child.

- An (un)curriculum sees everything as a learning opportunity.

- In an (un)curriculum, the job of the caregiver is to see learning moments and make the most of them, building on the child's prior knowledge and life experience.

- An (un)curriculum is based on children's needs, likes, and interests.

- In an (un)curriculum, great care is taken by adults to ensure that all aspects of the program are geared toward supporting the unique needs of individual children.

- An (un)curriculum supports children's autonomy.

- In an (un)curriculum, children are trusted as learners.

- A commitment to play is the defining feature of an (un)curriculum.

You can learn more about this in our book *Let Them Play: An Early Learning (Un)Curriculum*.

What are the four Ts and why are they important?

The four Ts are:

- Tasks—what children choose to do to engage themselves
- Time—how children choose to spend their time
- Technique—how children choose to perform tasks
- Team—who children choose to associate with

The four Ts are important because by giving children control of these elements, you show them they are trusted as capable, thinking, engaged learners. Author Daniel H. Pink argues in his book *Drive: The Surprising Truth about What Motivates Us* that adults who have control of the four Ts are happier and productive workers. The same goes for children—the four Ts are empowering.

How will this book help me support social development and other learning?

The activities and projects in this book are social lubricants that stimulate play, interaction, and conversation. These things lead to learning. As children engage with the ideas we put forth in this book, they also engage with each other and the world around them—which leads to learning.

What ages are the projects and activities in this book designed for?

We recommend them for kids in the two-and-a-half to six-year-old age range. Slightly younger and older kids will enjoy them as well, although you may need to make modifications based on the developmental level of the children.

How should the projects and activities in this book be introduced to kids?

We recommend simply *plopping* the opportunities into the children's environment. We introduced the term *plop* in our book *Let Them Play*. Plopping is the act of placing an activity, opportunity, or idea into an early learning environment so that children can discover it, play with it, explore it, and learn from it on their own, in their own way. You can plop things in the middle of the room for easy and immediate discovery, or you can plop them on a shelf for eventual discovery. Plops can happen any time of the day and in any place. The key is to step back and observe once you've plopped the plop. Note that just because something is plopped does not guarantee children will choose to engage with it.

Why should I step back?

The simple act of giving kids some space and not hovering shows them you trust them as competent and capable learners. We recommend you step back and allow the children to lead their own play, exploration, and discovery. You also put yourself in a great position to observe the unique curriculum that flows from each child. How far you step back depends on things like how old the children are, how well you know them, how tired or hungry they are, how many of them there are, how well they know each other, and what materials are involved. For example, you can back off a lot more with a pair of schoolagers who have played together since they were three years old than you can with a half-dozen hungry and tired toddlers. Stepping back does not mean abandoning the children. You need to be nearby to ensure their safety and support their play as needed.

How should I organize the kids when we do a new activity?

We suggest you allow for child-led self-organization whenever possible. Back in the day, kids were good at self-organizing ("bubble gum, bubble gum, in a dish…"). Trust kids with this task and support their efforts as needed.

How involved should kids be with preparing the projects?

As involved as possible. Let the kids lead. Allow them to own the *doing*. The more they do, the more they learn.

What if kids do it wrong?

Don't worry if kids take the activities we suggest in different directions. The activities are starting points, and there is no wrong way for their play to unfold. Remember, play is in the child, not the toy. Kids will bring their own experience, thought processes, creativity, and knowledge base to the materials. That means play can unfold in lots of different ways. We suggest you step back and enjoy the journey while ensuring everyone's health and safety. Let play evolve. Embrace spontaneity, throw caution to the wind, and go with it! No matter where they take the play, children will learn something of value.

What if I get a feeling a child is experiencing some sort of developmental delay?

If you feel a child is experiencing some sort of delay in their development, speak up. Talk to the child's parent, voice your concern, and take advantage of community resources that support families in this situation.

How can I support kids who are new to child-led play and exploration?

Here are a few simple ideas:

- Pair them with an older child who has lots of play experience.
- Model play for the child yourself.
- Remember the value of baby steps. Help the child ease into self-led play.
- Offer encouraging words and supportive conversation when they try new things. ("I like how you tried the fingerpaints. How did it feel to paint with your fingers?" or "I see you were building with the cardboard boxes. What were you making?")

Why are some of the book's activities just for adults?

We feel it is important for adults who live and work with children to step back from time to time and think about their process and practices—to contemplate their policies and choices—so we included chapters that we see as thought adventures for adults. It is good to take time once in a while to think about how you approach different topics. Look at these chapters as starting points for evaluating your approach to the topics discussed.

What are baby steps and why should I take them?

Baby steps are small, slow, mindful steps. Many times we adults want to rush in and make big changes or try lots of new things when we are exposed to new ideas.

This can often lead to chaos, leave us feeling overwhelmed, and end in frustration. When we encourage baby steps, we are asking that you slow down and be mindful about the way you introduce new play opportunities.

How else can I support child-led play?

Here are a few suggestions:

- Stay out of the limelight. Don't make yourself the center of the children's attention or take over the play. Be close enough to offer support and to ensure safety, but far enough away that the kids don't feel like you're hovering.

- Be organized. Know where your materials are and be able to get to them when they're needed. Part of your job is anticipating what the children *may* ask for so you can grab it in an instant when the children *do* ask for it.

- Focus on the experience. Don't get too wrapped up in trying to ensure that kids are developing specific skills. Early learning is about shared experiences and emotional relationships, so focus on the experiences these projects and activities provide rather than on any one skill set, concept, idea, or fact. In the long run, we seldom remember the moments we learned specific skills or facts. If we remember anything about our learning, we remember the experience—who we were with, what we were doing, or how the new idea or concept clicked in our head.

- Observe and document. Take photos and video and even capture audio recordings of kids involved in play so you can share what they learn with the parents in your program.

Do you offer any ongoing support for people trying to create (un)curriculums and support child-led play?

Sure we do. We feel it is our job to support our readers after they finish our books. Check out the conclusion to learn how to connect with us. We would love to hear from you.

Now go play!

Choice

Overview

It could be argued that learning to make mindful choices is one of the primary purposes of childhood. Throughout human history children have traditionally played at the work of the adults in their community—hunter, gatherer, caregiver, leader, healer—and in turn at the choice making these adults engage in. ("The wind is coming from the north. I need to loop around the forest and approach the wild boar in the clearing from the south so he is less likely to smell me coming.") In addition to playing at adult choice making, children have traditionally had opportunities for more real choice making in their own lives. Throughout most of human history, adults have been too busy with things like finding food, shelter, and water and defending their families from danger to pay much attention to their children, let alone turn into *helicopter parents*. There was not a lot of parental hovering in the thirteenth century, and that meant kids were trusted with making real choices from a very early age.

Over the past fifty years, opportunities to play at adult choice making and to experience real-world choice making have dwindled for children. In some cases, children are now told what to do, when to do it, and how it is to be done by well-meaning adults throughout the whole of their days. "Sally, it's time for you to put the baby dolls away and move to the block area with Kenny. Remember, you two: no throwing blocks, and no towers taller than your waist. That's just too dangerous."

The problem with this decrease in child choice is that kids who don't have much practice making choices turn into young adults who don't have much experience making choices. Finally finishing school and entering the *real world* become overwhelming for young people faced with the onslaught of decisions that come with adulthood.

The human brain is an apparatus, first and foremost, for dealing with the social environment.

—Judith Rich Harris, *The Nurture Assumption: Why Children Turn Out the Way They Do*

Why It's Important

Life is a never-ending series of choices: "Should I eat this donut or this carrot?" "Paper or plastic?" "Sleep in or get to work early?" "Drive in this storm or wait for it to pass?" Childhood is prime time for practicing at such decisions.

When adults, no matter how well intentioned, always make decisions for a child, the child misses out on chances to practice decision making—as well as to learn from the consequences of his choices, good and bad. Becoming good at making choices can take a lot of practice, and we hinder children when we limit their opportunities.

Not allowing children to make their own choices also impacts their sense of self, their feelings of control over their own lives, their autonomy, and their need for power. These things can cause stress and lead to behavior problems. Kids who feel they have no control over their choices often act out defiantly as a way to gain some control and power. The choices we make for ourselves as adults chart the entire course of our lives. It's important to support children as they learn to make theirs.

How to Support It

You can support children's choice making in your early learning setting by taking these actions:

1. Provide large blocks of time where children are free to make their own choices about what and how they play.

2. Create opportunities for real-world choice making. This can be as simple as letting a child decide whether she needs to wear a hat when she heads outside to play.

3. Trust their choices. Allowing a child to make a choice and then talking the child out of it because you don't agree with it undermines the child's choice making. Obviously, you have to step in and be the adult in situations involving real danger ("No, you can't jump from the second-story window with that paper parachute duct-taped to your back!"), but holding your tongue and trusting them to own their choices—good and bad—will help children learn to make better decisions.

4. Allow mistakes. Learning to make good choices requires making some bad choices—and then living with the consequences. This could mean allowing a child to have cold ears for a while when he chooses not to wear a hat out to play on a chilly day.

Questions to Ask Yourself

1. How do you feel when you notice that other people are taking control of choices that affect your life?

2. Which of your choices hinder kids from making more of their own choices?

3. What three things can you change in your early learning setting to support more child-led choice?

Notes

_____

_____

_____

_____

_____

_____

_____

Now continue on to the next chapter, and flow down a river of foil...

Foil Rivers

Overview

In this project, kids create rivers using aluminum foil and water and then splish and splash as they float items down the channels they've created. Constructing foil rivers requires plenty of cooperation, self-regulation, and problem solving. It's also a play-based opportunity to learn some physical-science concepts and practice language skills.

Ingredients

☐ aluminum foil (the heavy-duty stuff is best)

☐ floaties—stuff to sail down the foil river: paper scraps, tissue, flower petals, bits of yarn, and so on

☐ water

Process

1. Rip a long length of foil from the roll.

2. Lay the foil on an inclined surface. Driveways work great.

3. Carefully fold the long sides of the foil over on themselves a few times to create edges for the river as pictured on the next page.

4. Add water and floaties, step back, and let the kids play.

Let Them Own Discoveries

Resist the urge to show. Stop demonstrating how. Trust your littles (a.k.a. child care crew) to figure out what to do with whatever new, bright, and shiny object has been plopped in their environment. Owning discoveries is empowering. Empowered children try new things, aren't afraid to fail, think outside the box, wonder, make predictions, and have a strong sense of self.

More Play Adventures

- Build dams. Foil, clay, mud, and other materials can be used to dam and change the course of a foil river.

- Add color. Use liquid watercolor or food coloring to add color to your foil river.

- Construct a lake. Challenge children to use foil to build a lake for their river to flow into.

- Try tributaries. See if kids can make two, three, or more small rivers flow into a big river.

- Fabricate waterfalls. Can the kids figure out how to add a waterfall or two to their foil river?

Notes

_____

_____

_____

_____

_____

_____

_____

Try delaying gratification. See if you can hold off turning the page for five minutes…

Delayed Gratification

Overview

The ability to delay gratification is related to other self-regulatory skills, like impulse control and patience. The ability to delay gratification is one of the skills that make up *executive function*: the skills that allow us to think, act, and solve problems. Delayed gratification is a topic that has been studied a lot, most notably by psychologist Walter Mischel. Google *Stanford marshmallow test* to learn more about his work, or better yet, search the phrase on YouTube for some hilarious videos of kids trying not to eat marshmallows that will highlight how hard it is to delay gratification.

The ability to put off gratification has a direct impact on our relationships with others. For example, it is not socially acceptable to punch your best friend in the throat and take her dessert—no matter how yummy her piece of cake looks.

This is a skill that becomes easier with age—if you watch some marshmallow test videos, you will see that young children have almost no willpower when it comes time to not gobble up the marshmallow placed in front of them—but it is also something we can practice when we're young.

Why It's Important

Learning to delay gratification is important because in the adult world delaying gratification is required as we struggle to accomplish tasks and reach goals. There is no accomplishment or perseverance without the ability to delay gratification.

How to Support It

You can help children learn to delay gratification by taking these actions:

1. Provide them with opportunities to wait for things they desire. For example, help kids put off a chance to play with an exciting new Bright Shiny Object (BSO) until after the mess in the playroom is picked up.

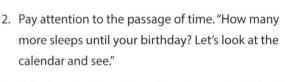

2. Pay attention to the passage of time. "How many more sleeps until your birthday? Let's look at the calendar and see."

3. Talk about it. Have discussions about what it feels like to wait for something you want. ("I was so excited to go to the movie last night, but it did not start until 7:00, and I had to wait and wait. All that waiting made me feel bouncy inside, and I could barely stand it!")

4. Avoid rewards. Handing out stickers or other prizes to children who succeed at delaying gratification makes it difficult for the child to develop intrinsic motivation (that is, motivation that comes from within the child, not from the outside world) and an internal locus of control (or the belief that events in one's life are caused by controllable factors like attitude and effort). Instead, children focus on the external rewards and become dependent on them.

5. Pay attention to their play. You will notice that children play at gratification delay in their dramatic play. (Overheard during dramatic play: "No, daughter, you have to wait to eat the birthday cake until after we sing to you." "You have to have three more sleeps before we can go to grandma's house." "Batman has to wait to attack until Superman recovers from the Kryptonite.") When you see this happening, look for opportunities to support and build on the play.

Questions to Ask Yourself

1. How do you feel when you have to delay gratification?

2. What memories do you have from your childhood about delaying gratification?

3. What can you change in your program to help children practice delaying gratification?

Notes

_____

_____

_____

_____

_____

_____

_____

_____

Just look to the next page for Ping-Pong ball–based prenumeracy and literacy skills…

Catch It!

Overview

This play opportunity involves a couple of kids, a chair, a cup, Ping-Pong balls, and a hunk of plastic rain gutter. It's a chance for pairs of kids to practice teamwork and problem solving through trial and error. The activity is also great for developing children's visual planning and visual tracking skills (vital literacy and numeracy skills).

Ingredients

- ☐ chair
- ☐ Ping-Pong balls
- ☐ plastic cup
- ☐ four-foot-long section of plastic rain gutter

Process

1. Set up the section of rain gutter as a ramp by placing one end on the seat of a chair and the other end on the floor. Make sure you have ample open floor space at the bottom of the ramp.

2. Set out the Ping-Pong balls and a plastic cup.

3. Ask a child to roll a ball down the ramp, and then demonstrate how to catch it with a cup.

4. Fade into the background, observe, and document the learning.

5. Note: You have the option to provide lots of ramps, cups, and balls so all the children can play at once. You also have the option to create some scarcity so that the children will have to figure out how to cooperate. Both options lead to social learning.

More Play Adventures

- Forget the ramp. The ramp is really not 100 percent necessary. Children can just roll the balls across the floor for their partners to catch.

- Adjust the angle. Changing the angle of the ramp changes the activity: steep ramps make for fast-moving balls, and gentle slopes make for easy-to-catch balls. You can demonstrate this or let the kids figure it out for themselves.

- Try different ramps. Instead of a rain gutter ramp, try this activity using a shower curtain, tablecloth, cardboard tube, or piece of wooden cove molding.

- Try different balls. Use bouncy balls, wooden balls, tennis balls, or marbles.

- Think up more catching play. If your littles are really into catching things, brainstorm other ways to play at catching.

- Common catching: You can catch with a parachute, a sheet, a towel, your shirt, or your hands. Have fun with the objects you're catching. Perhaps start with something easy, like a big stuffed teddy bear. Choose increasingly smaller items to throw and catch.

Notes

_____

_____

_____

_____

_____

_____

_____

Go to the next chapter and see if your expectations are met…

Expectations

Overview

The pressure to achieve and push to formal academics that comes with initiatives like No Child Left Behind and Race to the Top have left us expecting a lot from young children. For example, in many corners of the early learning world, infant and toddler curricula are now an expectation. There was a time, not too long ago, when babies were actually allowed to be babies and did not need adults pushing them to learn in accordance with a well-planned course of study.

As children get older, the expectations only get more intense. Kindergartners are now expected to start school ready to learn things that were part of the second half of first grade a decade or so ago, which means the expectations we used to have for five-year-olds are pushed down onto three-year-olds. The problem, of course, is that three-year-olds are not five-year-olds. The downward push of curriculum is not only developmentally inappropriate, but it is also ethically wrong.

For example, three-year-olds are wired to move and engage the world with their whole bodies; they are social creatures who are driven to move, touch, and talk. Expecting them to sit still, be quiet, and keep their hands to themselves is both a developmentally inappropriate expectation and an unethical one.

What's the alternative?

As early learning professionals, we need to take a collective deep breath, turn down the pressure, and flip our focus. Instead of concentrating on what *we* expect from children, we should pay attention to the things *they* expect from us. Things like safety, security, love, trust, and the freedom to lead their own learning. Bev Bos has said, "The child is the curriculum." As professionals, all of our expectations of a given child should flow from that child's unique interests, experiences, and needs.

Let Them Be Bored

Somewhere along the way, boredom got a bad rap. For some reason, well-intentioned adults feel the need to overschedule children's lives and make sure children are entertained every second. But we like boredom. It sparks creativity. Children who have time to be bored will use their imaginations to think outside the box and invent something new. Respect and trust young children enough to allow them plenty of time to be bored, plenty of time to use their brains and their resources to do something constructive, and plenty of time to ask for what they need to accomplish whatever task they come up with to move beyond boredom.

Why It's Important

Attending to the expectations of the children in our care is important because it helps them feel safe, secure, loved, respected, and trusted—all things the child needs to settle in, relax, and feel comfortable enough to engage in their environment and learn from what it has to offer. Children who are not comfortable in their environments are always on guard and never quite secure enough to completely let down their defenses. Children who are under constant bombardment by the

expectations of others tend to feel the same way, especially when the expectations are beyond their abilities. This can lead to learned helplessness—kids just quit trying.

How to Support It

1. Push back when you are pressured to push children to meet developmentally inappropriate expectations. Children cannot stand up for themselves and need you to defend them.

2. Create healthy emotional environments for the children in your care. Attend to their physical and emotional expectations and needs.

3. Be assured that when we urge you to pay attention to the expectations of children, we are not saying a child who expects a pony in the yard and a seventy-two-inch flat screen in the playroom should get a pony and new TV. The expectations we are concerned with fall under the heading of *needs*, not *wants*.

4. Pay attention to the unique curriculum that flows from each child and do your best to support it.

Questions to Ask Yourself

1. What two baby steps can you take to help push back against unrealistic expectations of the children in your care?

2. When have you pushed developmentally inappropriate expectations on children in the past, and how can you avoid such situations in the future?

3. How can you support the curriculum that emerges from each of the children in your care?

_____

_____

_____

_____

_____

_____

_____

Stretch out a bit before checking out the next chapter. You'll need to be loose...

Loose Parts Play

Overview

There was a day, back when kids had more free time and freedom to roam, when garages, sheds, and barns were scoured for loose parts—discarded lumber for tree forts, old bicycle wheels for go-carts, a little of *this* and some of *that* for dramatic play props. Such opportunities are lost to many children these days, but you can re-create the benefits of such scavenging by supporting loose parts play in your play area. Human brains like novelty, so curating an ever-changing collection of BSOs will keep kids entertained and learning for a long time. The collection will initiate countless social play scenarios and learning opportunities.

Ingredients

- ☐ bits
- ☐ pieces
- ☐ odds
- ☐ ends
- ☐ whatchamacallits
- ☐ doodads
- ☐ thingamajigs
- ☐ whatsits

Process

1. Curate a collection of loose parts and BSOs that will catch the attention of kids. Lumber, discarded pots and pans, pieces of plastic hose, copper wire, milk crates, plastic pipe, rope, and other found objects and castoffs are a starting point. Add as many BSOs to the collection as you have room to store.

2. Make your collection accessible.

3. Let children lead the play. Don't jump in too soon with your own ideas and suggestions. Be concerned about safety issues, but don't leap in and disrupt the play unless absolutely necessary.

More Play Adventures

• Change it up. Over time, even open-ended items like those in your collection can lose their appeal. To keep a loose parts collection interesting, add new items from time to time and rotate other items in and out. If an interesting whatsit has not been available for a while, the kids will be excited to see it when it comes back into play.

- Provide small parts. Curate a collection of small loose parts—nuts, bolts, wire, string, washers, and found objects—for tabletop play.

- Supply loose cardboard. Build a collection of cardboard boxes and cardboard sheets for children to play and create with. Expand the play opportunities by offering up plenty of tape, scissors, and markers.

- Provide tools. Loose parts will inspire a desire to build. Provide tape measures, hammers, pliers, and other tools to help support this desire.

- Support planning. Make sure kids have access to paper, pencils, clipboards, measuring sticks, and other materials to help in planning, labeling, and documenting their creations.

Notes

Want to access the next chapter? Just look to the next page…

Open Access

Overview

If the work of children is indeed to play, then the work of early educators is to ensure that children have open access to the tools they need to do their work. Children need free and open access to playdough, clay, scissors, baby dolls, Lego blocks, construction paper, glue, cardboard boxes, dirt, trucks, water, dress-up clothes, pipe cleaners, sticks, and all the other open-ended odds and ends we know children learn from.

In some cases, there is a tendency to hide these items away until the adult deems them appropriate. For example, in some programs children are not allowed near a pair of scissors until after they turn three. We have even heard of programs that consider playdough a "kindergarten toy."

In other cases, some items are hoarded and kept under lock and key. "Our budget is tight. If we use the glue, we will run out of glue and not be able to buy more glue, so we are not going to use any glue at all."

In still other cases, there is a lack of understanding about what materials kids need to do their work and what materials are safe for them to use. In these situations the materials are not provided or are actively banned. It happens with everything from cardboard boxes to sticks.

Abilities essential for academic success and productivity in the workforce, such as problem solving, reasoning, and literacy, all develop through various kinds of play, as do social skills such as cooperation and sharing.

—Susan Linn, *The Case for Make Believe: Saving Play in a Commercialized World*

Why It's Important

Simply put, kids can't do their work if they don't have the tools they need. Roofers can't roof without ladders, utility knives, and hammers. Surgeons can't perform surgery without sterile rooms, scalpels, and clamps. Kids can't play and learn without mud, blocks, and other open-ended materials.

How to Support It

1. Don't be stingy with materials. A supply closet full of glue and glitter is not doing anyone any good when it's locked away. Don't hoard it, use it.

2. Create flexible play spaces that children can freely alter to meet their needs. For example, dramatic play spaces set up in a traditional kitchen layout tend to be less engaging and flexible than a space with lots of generic furniture, cardboard boxes, and other open-ended materials.

3. Make it accessible. Arrange your space so that children have direct access to as many different materials and supplies as possible. This promotes their independence, shows that the adults in the room are

trusting, helps the children build self-control, and allows the children to freely follow their internal curricula.

Note: Many adults worry that giving kids free access to consumable supplies will result in wasted materials. Our personal experience and observations and anecdotal reports from other caregivers indicate that this is not the norm. There may be a lot of consumption when children are first exposed to openly accessible supplies, but as they get used to the idea, they tend to use only what they need. For example, Jeff was observing a just-turned three-year-old in a Toronto program as she painted in a well-stocked craft area. At one point she stopped painting, pulled open a drawer holding about a billion googly eyes, selected two, and added them to her painting.

Questions to Ask Yourself

1. How can you change your play space over time to support open access to materials?

2. What stresses you out about the idea of open access? How can you manage this stress?

3. Do you feel a need to hoard, restrict, or deny access to certain materials? Why?

Notes

_____

_____

_____

_____

_____

_____

Hurry! The next chapter is totally tubular to the max!

Funnel and Tube Frame

Overview

This simple frame adds variety to water-table play—and all the social interactions that take place during such play. The frame doesn't just support plastic tubes and funnels. It supports the exploratory and dramatic play kids engage in while using it.

Ingredients

- ☐ cedar two-by-four, 8 feet long (pressure treated or redwood two-by-four lumber is also acceptable)
- ☐ drill with the following bits: ⅛-inch drill bit, 1-inch spade bit, 1¼-inch spade bit, and a screwdriver bit
- ☐ wood glue
- ☐ saw (most any saw will work: handsaw, chop saw, table saw, skill saw, band saw)

- ☐ 2½-inch screws (stainless steel or exterior grade)
- ☐ clear plastic tubing (thin-walled tubing is more flexible and therefore easier for children to manipulate)
- ☐ plastic funnels
- ☐ water

Process

Part One: Construction

1. Cut the following pieces from the two-by-four: one 32-inch piece, two 16-inch pieces, two 12-inch pieces.

2. Attach a 16-inch piece to each end of the 32-inch piece using glue and screws. Use the ⅛-inch drill bit to drill pilot holes.

3. Attach the 12-inch pieces to the 16-inch pieces. Use the ⅛-inch drill bit to drill pilot holes.

4. Use the spade bit to drill holes in the uprights and crosspiece.

Part Two: Play

1. Show children that the holes in the frame support funnels and tubing.

2. Let them install the funnels and tubing as they wish, and let the water play begin.

More Play Adventures

- Use the frame in sand play. Kids will also enjoy using the frame, funnels, and tubes during sand play.

- Add some bungee cords. If you would like to use tubing that does not fit through the holes you drilled, you can use bungee tie-down straps to attach them. This makes it possible to use, for example, old vacuum cleaner hoses during sand play. Cable ties (zip ties) are another alternative for attaching big tubing.

- Customize the size. You can change the dimensions of the frame to fit your needs. For example, you could build one with a larger cross section that would fit across your whole sandbox.

- Get dramatic. Place the frame, funnel, and tubing in your dramatic play area and see what kind of play unfolds.

Notes

_____

_____

_____

_____

_____

_____

_____

Put on your Play Face for the next chapter…

Rough-and-Tumble Play

Overview

To some, rough-and-tumble play seems loud, chaotic, violent, and overly aggressive. It looks like fighting, and because they don't want kids to fight—or grow up to be violent—they feel that discouraging or banning such play is the right course of action.

The problem, however, is that play fighting is *play fighting*. It isn't real fighting. There is no evidence that kids who play aggressively when they are little will grow up to be violent adults, just like there is no evidence that children who put baby dolls in the play kitchen oven will grow up to cook their children.

The truth is that rough-and-tumble play is full of rich learning opportunities not readily available in other types of play. For example, it is a way for children to practice social cuing and to learn how to read body language, as well as a way to hone small- and large-muscle control, kinesthetic awareness, visual-tracking skills, balance, and more. It is also a chance to play with complicated concepts like power, leadership, strength, control, death, winning, losing, fear, and camaraderie. According to *The Art of Roughhousing: Good Old-Fashioned Horseplay and Why Every Kid Needs It* by Anthony T. DeBenedet and Lawrence J. Cohen, "Roughhousing activates many different parts of the body and the brain, from the amygdalae, which process emotions, and the cerebellum, which handles complex motor skills, to the prefrontal cortex, which makes high-level judgments. The result is that every roughhousing playtime is beneficial for body and brain as well as for the loftiest levels of the human spirit: honor, integrity, morality, kindness, and cooperation." Rough-and-tumble play is also a safe way for young children—usually boys—to show affection for each other. It's not always socially easy for a four-year-old boy to give a buddy a hug and say "I care about you man," but grabbing him in a bear hug and wrestling him to the ground can convey the same message (boys are weird).

When they engage in this type of play, children put on their Play Face (we got the term from our podcast buddy Lisa Murphy—she got it from someone else). A Play Face is friendly and open, with eyes big and bright. Kids might try to hide their Play Face with scowls and grimaces as part of their play, but "I'm here to play" might as well be written across their foreheads with a marker. During rough-and-tumble play, kids work very hard to keep the play balanced and moving forward—stronger kids hold back a bit, smaller kids put their all into the play. The goal is not harm. The goal is to keep the play moving. It can look and sound very violent, but the children engaged in the play are taking part in a dynamic, predominately nonverbal exchange of information meant to keep Play Faces from clouding over. All of this practice is useful in later life. For example, being able to read your spouse's or boss's face well is a valuable skill.

Let Them Manage Conflict

Too often, early childhood environments are overcontrolled to the point where all conflict has been removed. Whether that control comes in the form of making sure there is always one supply for each child or in the form of a teacher who always stops the conflict before it happens, preventing children from experiencing conflict does them no favors. How can a young child possibly learn how to handle conflict if she is never given the opportunity to practice? A loving early learning environment is the perfect setting for conflict-management lessons. Authentic experiences where a child's thoughts are respected and she is allowed to try different techniques to handle different types of conflict will benefit the child for life.

Why It's Important

It's important to find ways to support rough-and-tumble activities because most kids go through a developmental phase where they need to engage in this type of play. If such play is limited, banned, or made taboo, kids look for other outlets. For example, not allowing children to do play fighting can lead to children doing real fighting.

How to Support It

1. Create some rough-and-tumble friendly guidelines. For example, some programs have had success with *safe words* that kids use to stop the play when they feel overwhelmed, and others work to create a program culture where opting out of such play is easy.

2. Create a rough-and-tumble play space. Designating space for this type of play goes a long way toward keeping it safe and keeping it from disrupting other types of play. When you set up such a space, think about ways to provide padded surfaces, to deaden noise, and to avoid sharp edges.

3. Educate parents. Spell out in your handbook why rough-and-tumble play is developmentally appropriate and beneficial, and explain how you will work to keep it safe and to avoid injuries. We have also found that getting parents to think back to this type of play in their own childhood can be helpful. You should also make time for ongoing conversations about rough-and-tumble play and be available to discuss parent concerns.

Questions to Ask Yourself

1. If you dislike this kind of play, can you list the reasons for your dislike? Can you separate your personal dislike of such play from the need some children have to engage in it?

2. Did you engage in rough-and-tumble play as a child—even once? If so, what do you remember?

3. How can you use your own memories to help educate parents in your program about rough-and-tumble play?

Notes

_____

_____

_____

_____

_____

_____

_____

The next chapter is a bit of a stretch...

Stretch and Pop

Overview

We understand that because this activity involves balloons, it's likely to be banned, considered too dangerous for some early learning programs. We think that's silly and encourage folks to do it. See, the only way kids learn to assess real risk and recognize real danger is to have some experience with those things. Kids learn how to be careful and responsible with balloons by interacting with balloons. This bit of balloon play leads to abundant social interaction and learning. It can help kids learn a good deal about math, spatial relations, cause-and-effect relationships, and other good stuff as well.

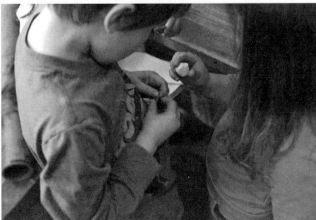

Denita Has an Idea I

During a discussion with kids after reading *The Mitten* by Jan Brett, one of my littles said, "Hey, a balloon stretches like a mitten!" I acted on his comment, quickly grabbing an unblown-up balloon and asking the children what they thought could possibly fit inside it. They gathered random toys and squeezed them inside the balloon as I held it open.

The children collaborated, took turns, tested hypotheses, shared ideas, and thought outside the box as they stuffed bizarre items into the balloon. There was a lot of discussion, trial and error, and problem solving: "Nope, this won't fit. It's waaay too big." "Whoa! I can't believe that fit. Look at how much the balloon is stretching!" "Hey! It looks like an X-ray when you hold it up to the light!"

The next day, we extended the fun and learning. I plopped mini animal erasers and more unblown-up balloons and handed ownership of the entire activity over to the children. They had to work together because not one of them could hold a balloon open *and* fill it at the same time. Math skills were brought into the learning as the children kept track of how many animal erasers were inside. Dramatic play scenarios unfolded. Spontaneous sorting and classifying of objects occurred. The children were so busy with balloon stuffing and all the play that evolved from it that they didn't get around to popping a balloon, so the contents could fly about, until the second day.

Ingredients

☐ balloons (Invest in decent balloons. The real cheap ones tend to rip easily when stuffed with stuff.)

☐ random loose parts (Most anything from your early learning environment will work: cars, blocks, dollhouse people, markers. Avoid objects with pointy parts.)

☐ a nice, sharp balloon-popping pin

Process

1. Hold open a balloon, and let children stuff items into it.

2. Once the balloon is fairly full, blow it up and tie it off.

3. Experience the balloon: let the kids handle it, shake it a bit, and hold it up to a light source to see if they can identify items by their silhouettes.

4. Have a conversation about what will happen when the balloon pops: How will it sound? What will happen to the balloon? What will happen to the items in the balloon? How can we prepare for the POP?

5. Make sure everyone stands a few paces back, and then pop the balloon.

6. Pick up and discard the balloon shrapnel. This is a good time for some balloon safety discussion about how balloons (and broken balloon bits) do not belong in mouths except when they're being blown up.

7. Follow the children. Imaginative storylines about the POP may come up while the children hunt for balloon bits to discard and the items that were inside. Spontaneous sorting of the found objects could occur. Or the POP might be met with an immediate chorus of "Do it again!" Whatever happens, go with the flow.

8. If you repeat the process—and we expect you will—hand ownership over to the children. Let them work together to hold open the mouth of the balloon and force-feed the toys. Let them be in control of the POP. Let them lead the cleanup process.

More Play Adventures

- Get wet. Pop water balloons. (Jeff learned from experience that this is best done outside. His wife, Tasha, seemed a bit bothered by indoor water-balloon popping when he tried it.)

- Get colorful. Pop balloons that contain a few squirts of washable paint. (Tasha would also call this an outside activity.)

- Get muddy. See how much mud kids can stuff into a balloon. What happens when you blow it up and pop it? (You guessed it: Listen to Tasha and do this outside.)

- Pop other items. Try popping nonlatex gloves, paper sacks, bubbles, bubble wrap, or ziplock bags.

Notes

_____

_____

_____

_____

_____

_____

_____

The next chapter is full of suds for your buds…

Sudsational Play

Overview

This one involves water and cheap shampoo. These simple and open-ended materials are bursting with play possibilities and provide a jumping-off point for conversation, conflict, creativity, connections, innovation, exploration, imagination, and more. Kids will enjoy painting with suds, carrying suds, squeezing suds, making more suds out of suds, scrubbing with suds, pouring suds, wearing suds, walking in suds, and probably even eating some suds.

Ingredients

- ☐ water
- ☐ cheap shampoo
- ☐ plastic containers
- ☐ disposable foam paintbrushes of assorted sizes

Process

1. Plop a dollop of shampoo in the bottom of a plastic container. This is not rocket science; there's no need to measure.
2. Blast it with a jet of garden-hose water.
3. Set the paintbrushes by the container, step back, and see what kind of play unfolds.
4. Refresh the suds as needed.

More Play Adventures

- Roll on. Add some paint rollers to the activity. For more fun, duct-tape a wooden dowel or section of PVC pipe to the paint-roller handle. Manipulating a long-handled roller will require teamwork and cooperation.

- Chalk it up. Add some ground-up sidewalk chalk to the suds for colorful play.

- Add surprise. Hide toy dragons, fairies, dinosaurs, or other unexpected items in the suds.

- Add more color. Add liquid watercolor to the container before pouring in the water to create colorful suds play.

- Whip it. Add some old-fashioned, hand-crank egg-beaters. Even better, see what happens when you mix up some shampoo and water using an electric hand mixer.

- Go incognito. Let's face it. Suds make great beards. Make sure to have at least one mirror nearby, and take plenty of photos.

- Get dramatic. Provide suds for outside dramatic play.

- Let them loose. Provide assorted containers, spoons, cups, and other items to facilitate bubbly play.

_____

_____

_____

_____

_____

_____

_____

_____

What if you start reading the next page right now…

What If . . . ?

Overview

What if we let go of our curriculum-driven expectations for children and followed their lead? What if we trusted children enough to really step back and support them while they followed their internal curricula? What if we made more time and space in our programs for the children's *what if*s?

Children's *what if*s are windows to their internal curricula: "What if I was big and I was the mom?" "What if we brought the blocks outside and built up to the sky?" "What if we could mix paint with the playdough?" "What if we went up the slide part today and down the steps?"

Children's *what if*s do not, of course, always come in the form of "what if." Children voice their internal curricula in many ways ("Can I . . ." "Maybe we could . . ." "One day my sister got to . . ." "I saw this kid who . . ."). Adults need to pay attention to all the ways children voice their interests, desires, needs, and expectations.

Why It's Important

Paying more attention when children try to communicate with you will help you tune the play environment to their needs. Too often, adult schedules and curricula override the stated needs and interests of children. If we really believe that children are the curriculum—that they each have their own internal curricula guiding their learning—then we need to listen a bit more carefully when they try to express it with their questions and requests.

Children can find it difficult to assert their needs and interests. They are little and have very little *power* or *control,* which means they are not always skilled at voicing what's on their minds. They need us to slow down and pay attention.

47

How to Support It

1. Manage your stress. Our adult stress can often blind us to the needs of others. When we do not take care of our own needs, we have a hard time tuning in to the needs of the other people in our lives.

2. Slow down and pay attention to children's questions. The rush and tumble of our adult world often leads us to zip over questions and requests from children—and that can lead to missed opportunities to support their learning.

3. Create learning environments that are flexible enough to change easily based on the questions and interests the children bring to the space.

4. If you toss your own *what if* at a group of children, respect them enough to move on to other things if they are not interested. For example, if you suggest outside playtime ("How about we get this place picked up and then head outside?") and the kids would rather stay inside and continue at the play they are already engaged in, then stay inside.

Questions to Ask Yourself

1. Do you ever find yourself rushing past the questions and requests of children in order to stay on schedule or meet curriculum expectations?

2. Have you ever felt that someone in a position of authority was not paying attention to something that was important to you? If so, how did it make you feel?

3. Have you ever had a problem asserting yourself or conveying your needs to someone else? If so, how did this make you feel?

4. What small changes could you make to your existing play environment to make it more responsive to the questions and interests of the children who use the space?

Notes

_____

_____

_____

_____

_____

_____

_____

Flip the page, and we'll pump you up like Hans and Franz…

Pump Play

Overview

The most amazing ideas spring from the unfenced minds of young children. This chapter came about because the kids in Denita's program brought their imaginations and experiences along when they had an opportunity to play and explore with a couple dollar-store balloon pumps.

The children self-organized and immediately took the lead when they discovered the novel pumps Denita plopped into the play area. The result? Exploration, cooperation, discovery, problem solving, sorting, classifying, and more.

Ingredients

☐ hand-operated balloon pumps (water squirters work well too)

☐ small craft pom-poms

☐ Ping-Pong balls

Process

1. Plop the materials onto an activity table.

2. Step back.

3. Observe and be ready to support the play as it unfolds. Resist the urge to demonstrate how to use the balloon pumps. Let them figure it out and own the learning experience.

More Play Adventures

- Ramp up the play. Add a section of plastic rain gutter to the materials you've plopped. Kids usually turn the gutter piece into a ramp and blow items up or down it. Be prepared to follow their lead if your crew does something else.

- Dramatic pumps. Plop the pumps into your dramatic play area.

- Confetti cannon. Create a really small funnel with a piece of construction paper and a bit of tape. The narrow end should fit tightly over the nose of the pump. The wide end should measure an inch or so across. Fill the funnel with confetti or small bits of torn-up paper, and then blast it into the air. Mix in some glitter to add sparkle to your confetti cannon.

- Water pump. Add a few balloon pumps to water play, and see what the kids discover.

- Will it move? Have the kids gather a bunch of random items and then test to see if the items move when blasted with a balloon pump. Place the items that move in one pile and the ones that don't in another.

Let Them Struggle

A child is standing two feet from you, trying to zip his coat. He is grunting and making other Oscar award–winning "struggle" noises and facial expressions. He doesn't say a word, just keeps glancing to see if he has your attention.

Anyone who has young children in their lives is likely to know this scene well. It's ripe with learning potential, but how the adult handles it greatly affects the child's empowerment, perseverance, and sense of self-pride. *Let the child struggle.* Do not swoop in and do it for him. Do not put words into his mouth by saying, "Do you need help?" or worse, "Would you like me to zip that for you?"

Respect a child's right to struggle, respect his right to determine when it is time for help, respect his right to earn that Oscar. In due time, the child will either find success on his own, figure out that he needs help and you aren't going to offer unless he asks for what he needs, or break down in tears. All are worthy moments full of authentic learning.

- Racetrack. Draw a racetrack shape on a hunk of poster board or cardboard. Make sure you identify the track's starting point and finish line. Place a craft pompom on the starting line, and let the kids take turns blasting it around the track. As they play, the kids will probably develop their own rules for the activity. Follow their lead.

Notes

_____

_____

_____

_____

_____

_____

There's no need for suspense—check out the next chapter and see what we suspend…

The Suspended Branch of Play

Overview

Building a Suspended Branch of Play leads to a wide range of social play possibilities, experimentation, and learning. It's just a branch with some hooks and a Hula-Hoop that hangs from a tree, but the versatility of this project will make it a favorite of kids and adults.

Ingredients

- ☐ a branch approximately 4 inches in diameter and 4 feet long
- ☐ eight ¼-inch-by-3-inch screw hooks
- ☐ a drill with a ³⁄₁₆-inch wood bit
- ☐ double loop chain
- ☐ a tree with limbs of accessible height
- ☐ Hula-Hoop
- ☐ balls, beanbags, and other throwable items

Process

Part One: Construction

1. On one side of the branch drill a ³⁄₁₆-inch pilot hole about 4 inches from each end of the branch, and then twist a screw hook into each of the holes.

2. Rotate the branch 180 degrees and drill six evenly spaced ³⁄₁₆-inch pilot holes. Twist the six remaining screw hooks into these holes.

3. Use the double loop chain to suspend the branch from a sturdy tree limb so that it is 6 to 7 feet above the ground and parallel to the ground.

4. Hang the Hula-Hoop from the Suspended Branch of Play.

Part Two: Play

1. Place the throwables near the suspended Hula-Hoop.

2. Step back and let the children organize their own play.

Let Them Control the Learning

A child-led, play-based program is not an unstructured program. On the contrary, in order for children to successfully control their learning (which is what should happen in a child-led program), the adult needs to structure the environment so that boundaries are clear and reasonable, expectations are clear and reasonable, and consequences are clear and reasonable. When an early learning environment is properly structured, children can control the learning. The adult supplies the structure so the children can feel a sense of control. Feeling control over what they're doing, when they're doing it, how they're doing it, and whom they're doing it with is empowering for a young child. Children who feel a sense of control throughout their day will not go looking for socially inappropriate ways to gain control. Knocking over a friend's tower is full of control. Biting is full of control. Screaming, yelling, tantrums—all of these are ways children can gain control, if need be. Give young children a structured environment where they can be in control in a positive way.

More Play Adventures

- Suspended pulley play. Attach a pulley to one of the hooks. Thread a rope through the pulley. Tie a bucket to one end of the rope. Let the kids play and explore.

- Suspended weaving. Use bungee cords to attach a 4-foot section of wire shelving to the Suspended Branch of Play. Provide yarn, rope, string, flagging tape, pipe cleaners, and other items that the children can weave into the section of shelving. (The shelf can be hung vertically, horizontally, or diagonally for more play variations.)

- Suspended water play. Suspend flexible plastic tubing or old vacuum cleaner hoses from the hooks using bungee cords, and let children pour water into the tubes.

- Suspended PVC pipe play. In Jeff's book *Do-It-Yourself Early Learning,* he explains how to build a PVC construction set. If you've built such a set, use string to suspend a section or two of pipe from the hooks. Then let the kids build off those pipes with other bits and pieces from the construction set. And don't be surprised if this adventure leads to some pipe-based water play.

- Suspended pendulum. On the 4-inch side, drill a ½-inch hole about 1¼ inch from the edge of a 12-inch-long two-by-four. Secure one end of a ¼-inch rope to the board through the hole. Attach the other end of the rope to a hook so the board hangs a few inches from the ground. Let the kids explore the pendulum you've created as they play catch with it and knock things over with it.

- Suspended music play. Hang old pots, pans, cookie sheets, and muffin tins from the Suspended Branch of Play. Provide wooden dowels or sticks, and allow the children to tap, bang, and thump out some tunes.

- Suspended art. Drill ½-inch holes in two corners of a 2-by-4-foot piece of plywood. Use the holes and bungee cords to suspend the plywood from the Suspended Branch of Play. Tape some paper to the plywood. Provide paint, markers, colored pencils, and other crafty materials, and let the kids create.

- Watch the wind. Hang lots of ribbons or flagging tape from the hooks, and watch it blow in the wind.

- Listen to the wind. Hang wind chimes or cowbells from the hooks, and listen to them make music.

- Feed the birds. Hang store-bought or child-made bird feeders from the hooks, and watch the birds eat.

- Step up. Provide a step stool or a small ladder so the kids can climb up and reach the hooks, and put the loose parts you curated in chapter 6 nearby. Then step back, and let the play unfold.

Notes

_____

_____

_____

_____

_____

_____

_____

We don't want to push you, but just look to the next page and read on…

Self-Regulation

Overview

Over the past few decades, as the kindergarten curriculum has been pushed down into preschool classrooms, many early learning programs have become more focused on pushing children to attain a checklist of academic skills ("Can she count to one hundred? Check! Can she spell her name? Check! Has she stopped making the letter *s* backwards? Check!). In some settings, this push to formal academics has led to less focus on creating environments that help children learn self-regulatory skills. This means more and more children struggle with managing interpersonal interactions ("She did not say my headband was pretty today, so she is not my friend anymore!") and their own self-control ("He would not give me the blue paint, so I punched him!").

Included in the skills that make up *executive function* is self-regulation, or the ability to control one's impulses. It means being able to avoid doing things, even when you want to do them ("I'm not going to pull her hair"); to stop doing things, even when you do not want to stop ("His face tells me I'm being too aggressive—I'm going to back off a bit so his Play Face comes back"); and to start doing things, even when you do not want to start ("I hate carrying my plate to the kitchen, but I'm going to do it anyway"). Self-regulation is not the same as obedience. Self-regulated people behave the same whether an authority figure is looking or not. Self-regulated people are able to delay gratification and suppress impulses. They are able to visualize potential consequences for possible actions and consider alternative choices. Self-regulation involves both social-emotional and cognitive behaviors.

- -

In so many ways, learning is a fundamentally social act. From circle time in kindergarten, to study groups in college, to team projects in the work-force, sociability has always greased the gears of learning.

—Tony Bingham and Marcia Conner, *The New Social Learning: A Guide to Transforming Organizations through Social Media*

- -

Why It's Important

Self-regulation is important because the ability to manage yourself in the world is kind of important. It is also kind of something we will *all* be doing *all* our lives. If you poll a group of kindergarten teachers, you will find most would much rather start the school year with a room full of children who can wait their turn, delay gratification for a bit, and use the toilet without assistance than a room full of kids who *cannot* do those things, but who *can* count to a thousand, speak a bit of Russian, and read at a third-grade level.

How to Support It

1. Trust kids to do things on their own that they can do on their own. For example, let kids put on their own shoes or clean up their own mess after lunch—even if it is quicker and more efficient to do it for them.

2. Engage children in real-world work. For example, allow them to wipe tables after meals, help fold laundry, and sweep up the sand that was tracked in from the playground. These tasks help them learn responsibility.

3. Allow children to struggle with tasks and make mistakes. Learning to self-regulate requires learning to persevere, overcome obstacles, and move beyond failures and setbacks.

4. Let them play. Dynamic child-led play is filled with opportunities to practice self-regulatory skills.

Questions to Ask Yourself

1. Do you do things for kids that they could do on their own? If so, why?

2. Is your play environment more focused on children attaining academic skills than self-regulatory skills? If so, how can you make a few small changes that will change the focus?

3. How can you alter your daily schedule to support children in attaining and honing more self-regulatory skills?

Notes

_____

_____

_____

_____

_____

_____

_____

Kids will really be attracted to the next chapter's DIY project…

Magnet Mittens

Overview

Stitching magnets onto a pair of kid's mittens will lead to dramatic play about superpowers, aliens, wizards, monsters, robots, and more. Such dramatic play is rich in social learning, a great way for kids to expand their vocabularies, and a chance for them to test out their knowledge of how the world works in a nurturing environment.

Ingredients

- ☐ a few pairs of children's knit mittens
- ☐ needle and thread
- ☐ ½-inch ceramic magnets or magnetic hematite

Process

1. Place a few magnets on the finger areas of the mittens.

2. Stitch the magnets in place.

3. Make a few pair of magnet mittens, and then plop them into your play area for the children to discover.

More Play Adventures

- Add the thumb. You can sew a magnet onto the mitten's thumb too.

- Make magnet gloves. Place one magnet on each finger, and stitch them in place.

- Make a magnet hat. Hot glue a few magnets to the bill of a child's baseball cap.

- Make magnet socks. Stitch a few magnets onto the toes of some brightly colored socks.

Notes

_____

_____

_____

_____

_____

_____

_____

If it doesn't feel too risky, look to the next page and read on…

Risk Assessment

Overview

We live in a world where some adult factions work relentlessly to eliminate every conceivable risk in the lives of children. Blowing out birthday cake candles *could* spread disease, tree climbing *could* result in a broken bone, a four-year-old crossing a quiet residential street *could* be struck down by a speeding garbage truck, a shark attack *could* take place at the beach, that stranger *could* be a pedophile, and Josh *could* choke on those grapes and die.

The problem is that most *coulds* never happen. We've been unable to find any documentation showing that blowing out candles has resulted in a single transmission of disease. Very few kids who climb trees break arms. The vast majority

Let Them Lead

Are the children doing something that is unexpected? Take the time to reflect before you react. Ask yourself two simple questions: (1) Are they hurting anyone? (2) Are they hurting anything? If the answer is no, then let them lead.

Here's an example: Jenn, a family child care provider, had spray bottles filled with water for her crew. Her adult-minded plan? The children would spray different items around the yard and watch as the colors of rocks, cement, wooden fences, and so on changed. Much to her dismay, something unexpected happened. A child unscrewed the spray bottle. Jenn took the time to reflect before she reacted. She took a moment to understand what the child intended to do. She asked him, and he said he was making a flood. He had experienced the Missouri River flood firsthand, and that experience was now showing up in his play. His play was completely harmless. He was not hurting anyone or anything. He was simply doing something Jenn had not planned on or expected.

Reflect before you react. Let them lead.

of strangers are good people. And even if Josh starts choking on a grape, he will probably cough it up.

When it comes to risk, we adults need to take a breath, turn down the *fear*, and worry a bit less. When we see the world as a dangerous, out-to-get-you, never-safe, everything-is-a-threat place, that is the way children learn to see it too.

Once we turn down the fear a bit, we need to take some mindful steps to help children learn to assess and manage the real-world risks they encounter. Learning to mindfully assess and manage risk takes practice; it is a skill that has to be developed and practiced before it is mastered. In that sense, it is a lot like learning to walk: we start out without much skill or experience, and over time we practice, make mistakes, gain confidence, and master the process.

If we want children to possess the knowledge and judgment necessary to safely cross the street and determine where it is safe to climb and swim, then we need to help them pool a depth of life experience.

Why It's Important

Basic survival in the world requires that we humans learn to effectively assess and manage risks every day. Not providing opportunities to build skills and experience in this area makes navigating daily life difficult and scary—and it cuts into our feelings of self-worth and confidence.

How to Support It

1. Educate parents about the importance of helping children assess and manage risks. This can be done through a parent handbook and ongoing discussion as well as through the sharing of photos and videos of children at play.

2. Audit your play environment, and address any major risks to make the space safe for child-managed risks. For example, anchoring shelving units to walls in toddler rooms is a good idea because children of this age love to climb. If the shelving is secured, Kimmie might fall while trying to reach her favorite dinosaur, but she will not pull the shelf over on top of herself.

3. Arrange for managed risk taking. Remember, learning to manage risk requires opportunities to take risks. Managed risk taking can look like a rope to climb, a wall to scale, a strange puppy to meet, a street to cross, or a decision to make. Let children lead—and make mistakes—in these situations, but be near at hand to support them as needed.

Questions to Ask Yourself

1. Do you ever find yourself worrying about things that could maybe, possibly, potentially go wrong so much that you prevent children from engaging in certain activities at all?

2. In your experience, how does it feel to take a calculated risk and then learn that you can trust your own judgment?

3. As an adult, how hard would it be to take a calculated risk or to trust your own judgment without having the pool of experience you acquired in your youth?

_____

_____

_____

_____

_____

_____

_____

_____

Be careful; you could put an eye out with the next chapter…

Slingshots

Overview

Some see slingshots as risky, dangerous, and inappropriate for young children. We see them as a chance for children to practice self-control and social skills—as well as to hone reading skills, like visual tracking, and writing skills, like small-muscle control.

Ingredients

- ☐ Y-shaped branch between ½ inch and 1 inch in diameter and around 8 inches long
- ☐ two large rubber bands
- ☐ 1-by-3-inch hunk of durable fabric
- ☐ 4-inch cable ties
- ☐ aluminum foil

Process

1. Using a cable tie, secure one end of a rubber band to an upper arm of the Y-shaped branch. Do the same with another rubber band and cable tie on the other upper arm of the branch.

2. Attach the loose ends of the two rubber bands to opposite ends of the fabric using cable ties.

3. Crumple a hunk of aluminum foil into a ball.

4. Fire!

More Play Adventures

- Set some ground rules. Discuss slingshot safety with the kids, and come up with some guidelines for acceptable slingshot play. If the kids help make the rules, they'll be more apt to follow them.

- Add more rubber. You can beef up the power of your slingshot by adding another rubber band or two to each side.

- Make a target. The suspended Hula-Hoop described in chapter 14 makes a great one.

- Shoot for distance. See how far (or high) kids can launch their foil balls. Use a stick to demark a starting line, have everyone shoot from behind that line, and measure to see who shoots their foil ball the farthest.

- Shoot for accuracy. Set out a laundry basket, cardboard box, or plastic tote, and see who can fire a foil ball into it.

- Make a splash. Fire foil balls into a wading pool or other container of water. You can even set toy boats afloat to provide water-based targets.

- Add other targets. Providing a wide variety of targets helps keep slingshot-wielding kids from shooting at their peers and pets. Stuffed animals, plastic containers, tree trunks, toy dinosaurs, and other inanimate and shatterproof objects all make fine targets.

- Play tag. (Someone, probably a boy, will eventually come up with this use for the slingshot, so we figured we'd include it.) Everyone has a slingshot. There's one foil ball. Whoever's "it" fires the foil ball until hitting another player. The someone who got hit becomes "it." Repeat. (Jeff knows from experience that this is a fun game, but in his day, they played with a rock.)

- Try other ammo. We think the foil ball is the best ammo option, but go ahead and try other options. Be careful.

Notes

Say *Yes* to the next chapter, and see what we have to share…

19 Yes...And

Overview

It's easy for adults to fall into a *No* rut in early learning settings. When there is always someone who needs a body part wiped or washed, paperwork that has to be done, and a clock or posted schedule pushing everyone toward the *next thing*, adults often meet children's requests with *No*.

Most of us don't see ourselves as *No* people—we're fun loving, like trying new things, and enjoy adventure! But the stress, rush, and push of the job can change us all slowly over time, and one day we wake up and realize we're in a *No* rut.

The alternative to the *No* rut is *Yes...And*.

Yes...And is an improvisational comedy technique that affirms the contribution of one person and builds on it. The *Yes* says, "I'm meeting you where you're at." The *And* says, "Here's what I have to contribute to the situation." On stage, the *Yes...And* keeps the scene moving, shows a level of trust between the players, and sends everything in interesting directions. To see *Yes...And* in action, just check out reruns of the British or American version of *Whose Line Is It Anyway?*

In an early learning setting, *Yes...And* can also keep things moving, show trust, and lead in interesting directions. For example, the activities in this book are all starting points. When you try them out, if you respond to children's suggestions and requests with a *No*, not much is going to happen. If, on the other hand, you offer up a *Yes...And,* there's no limit to the adventures the children can have.

Young children may not be aware of the emotions they are experiencing. They may not yet understand the socially correct way to communicate them. The result is that your little one may act out in anger when he is actually sad, or she may just become grumpy for no apparent reason.

—**John Medina,** *Brain Rules for Baby: How to Raise a Smart and Happy Child from Zero to Five*

Why It's Important

Shutting kids down with *No* all the time devalues what they have to offer, doesn't show trust, and rejects their efforts to express their inner curricula. Taking advantage of *Yes…And* shows that you respect and value what they have to offer. It also provides you with opportunities to tailor the situation or environment to meet their needs.

How to Support It

1. Listen. There are times when adults are so busy or so deep in their own heads that they don't take the time to really listen to children. In fact, sometimes adults find themselves composing responses before children have even finished talking. Slow down, tune in, and invest time in actually listening to what children have to say before crafting a response. Then do your best to offer up a *Yes...And*.

2. Let go. Give up some adult control and ego. Go with the flow. Follow the children's lead.

3. Make decisions that avoid *No* and put forth ideas and solutions: "Yes, we can squirt some paint into the water play tote." "Sure, you can bring the baby dolls outside today." "Of course we can go for a walk after lunch."

4. See possibilities. Listening and letting go a bit will open your eyes up to the possibilities in children's requests and suggestions. Anticipate the value and learning potential in their requests, and offer up ways to support their visions.

5. Remember that *Yes...And* is a skill that has to be developed. It will be challenging at first but will get easier with practice.

6. Take a class. Consider taking an improv class or reading up on other improv techniques online.

Questions to Ask Yourself

1. Do you get in *No* ruts that shut down child-led play from time to time? If so, what triggers these ruts for you, and how can you avoid them?

2. How do you feel when you are shut down with a *No* and not supported? How do you feel when your ideas and suggestions are embraced and built upon?

3. What scares you about the idea of *Yes...And*?

Notes

_____

_____

_____

_____

_____

_____

_____

The next chapter really "socks" it to you…

Sock Sandbags

Overview

This one comes from way back in Jeff's youth. During games of war, he and his buddies created sandbags with old socks, sand, and rubber bands. They spent hours hauling the sandbags around, building walls, and waiting for enemy attacks. All that play was full of social learning, problem solving, conversation, and imaginative adventure.

Ingredients

- ☐ tube socks
- ☐ cable ties
- ☐ sand

Process

1. Fill socks with sand.

2. Secure sock openings with cable ties. Trim the tie tails.

3. Step back, and let the children stack, build, and create.

More Play Adventures

- Fluffy sock balls. Pick up a few pairs of brightly colored children's socks, loosely stuff them with fiberfill, secure the ends with cable ties, and trim the tie tails and any excess sock. Your fluffy sock balls are safe for kids to toss around inside. Kids will use them in games and in dramatic play.

Let Them Solve Problems

Give children ownership of problems.

- A four-year-old child dumps a bucket of toys right in the middle of the room, upsetting the play space of two other children, and they are not happy. She has a problem to solve.

- A child spills his milk. He has a problem to solve.

- A child comes running to you because someone took a toy away from her. She has a problem to solve.

Children may need coaching and support, but eventually they'll spread their wings and fix, or attempt to fix, their own problems. Opportunities to solve problems when they come up give kids life experience that comes in handy. It provides them with a history of experiences they can reflect on in similar situations and use to prevent future problems.

- Sock beanbags. Fill colorful children's crew socks with plastic pellets and secure with cable ties (trim the tie tails) to create your own beanbags.

- Sock dolls. Provide kids with socks, fiberfill, cable ties, scissors, and markers, and allow them to create sock dolls. Help the process along as needed.

- Get crafty. Use the sock beanbags as paint dabbers. Use white crew socks instead of colorful ones, and then let the kids dab them with paint and/or markers as they work.

- Sock puppets. This seems pretty obvious, but in our screen-filled world, it's likely many kids have never made a simple sock puppet. We're not going to give instructions, though. You'll figure it out.

Notes

_____

_____

_____

_____

_____

_____

_____

_____

Bubble gum, bubble gum in a book. Turn to the next chapter and take a look…

Child-Led Games

Overview

For the vast majority of human history, children were in control of their games. They picked the teams ("Bubble gum, bubble gum, in a dish. How many pieces do you…"), made the rules ("No kicking it over the fence! They have a mean dog."), enforced them ("Raise your hand if you think she was out! See? Everyone saw you get tagged!"), and changed things as needed to keep the play going ("Jaden has to go home. Kim, you have to switch teams so they will be even.").

This type of play was rich in learning. Children practiced and honed social skills, problem-solving skills, large- and small-muscle skills, and more.

Nowadays, most kid's games are at least partially adult controlled. Adults create the games and the rules (Battleship, Candy Land, Angry Birds, Little League baseball), pick the teams, set the schedules, run the practices, keep score, enforce the rules, design the uniforms, and more.

Back in the day, if kids wanted to play soccer, they grabbed a ball, found a mostly level lot without too much dog poop and broken glass, and got to playing. Now, they put on a uniform, ride in the back of a minivan (while watching a DVD) to a laser-leveled and well-manicured field, and then play by rules made by one set of adults and enforced by another set of adults.

Adults have taken so much control over children's games that in many situations winning and losing have been removed from the process. Some sports leagues do not keep score, and everyone gets a participation trophy.

In addition to taking control of children's games, some adults work to ban certain games because they feel they are too risky or are socially unacceptable. For example, dodgeball and tag are banned on many school playgrounds.

One way to promote social skills and learning in the modern world is to once again give kids ownership of their games.

Why It's Important

Games of all kinds offer children dynamic, real-time occasions to practice social skills, build thinking skills, improve physical skills, and self-regulate—all things they will use daily for the entirety of their lives. Taking away ownership of their games steals this learning.

Giving them control of their games is important because it gives back the associated learning opportunities. This is vital, because children need lots of practice with all the things mentioned above as well as opportunities to learn to win and lose graciously, work as part of a team, persevere, problem solve, and all the other things game play teaches.

How to Support It

1. Support children in inventing and playing their own games. If they have never done this, you will have to nurture the process.

2. Look for opportunities to let kids have more *power* and *control* in their games—customizing the rules of Monopoly or their favorite card game, for example.

3. Give them plenty of *time* and *space* to play—these elements often lead to on-the-fly game invention.

4. Allow boredom. Not having anything to do—freedom from adult direction—can lead to the creation of wonderful games and play scenarios.

5. Remember that games can take many forms, from freeze tag to go fish to house.

Questions to Ask Yourself

1. Have you ever found yourself taking control of a child's game when it would be just as easy to let them lead?

2. What small step could you take tomorrow to help the kids in your care own their own games?

3. What are your childhood memories about games? What did you learn?

Notes

_____

_____

_____

_____

_____

_____

_____

Sing as you turn the page: "Red Solo cup, kids will stack you up…"

Cup Blocks

Overview

Who knew that something as unassuming as a stack of plastic cups could generate so much learning? Kids will discover all sorts of ways to play and learn with these simple materials. They will enhance problem-solving skills, numeracy skills, literacy skills, muscle skills, and more with the ideas in this chapter.

An overemphasis on standardized tests in our schools is robbing children of genuine learning opportunities and resulting in the loss of unstructured play, arts activities, and social time, all of which are essential to their well-being. Childhood as we know it is being stolen from our children, and it is time for us, as concerned parents, grandparents, and citizens, to take it back.

—**Nancy Carlsson-Paige**, *Taking Back Childhood: A Proven Road Map for Raising Confident, Creative, Compassionate Kids*

Ingredients

☐ a variety of inexpensive, shatter-resistant plastic cups (Think dollar-store deal.)

Process

1. Plop the cups into your block area.

2. Step back and support the play as needed.

More Play Adventures

- Use disposable cups. Don't have space in your program to permanently add a bunch of cup blocks? Make this a once-and-a-while material by using paper or plastic disposable cups. They aren't as durable as their reusable cousins, but you get a lot of them for your money, and once they're beaten up by play, you can recycle them.

- Add more blocks. Cup blocks can be fun alone, but they become more fun and flexible when combined with other blocks.

- Ink them. Grab a Sharpie and add letters, words, and numbers to your cups. Kids who are interested will work these symbols into their play.

- Classify and count. If your cup blocks are different colors and/or shapes, you will probably find that kids start sorting them on their own. Kids will also use the cups for numeracy play: they will count them, they will place a stack of one cup next to a stack of two cups next to a stack of three cups and so on, and they will use the cups as receptacles when sorting other items.

- Fill them up. Imagine the awesome crash-and-splash sound a pyramid of water-filled cups will make when it tips over. Let the kids build that pyramid.

- Make mud blocks. Fill your cups with some nice thick mud. Invert the cups in a fairly shady area, and let the mud dry for a few days. The blocks of dried mud should slip from the cups. Now let the mud-block play begin.

- Make ice blocks. Fill cups with colored water and freeze. Then remove the ice blocks from the cups and play. Get creative and make multicolored ice blocks.

- Mix them. How about combining mud blocks and ice blocks for some slippery, messy play?

- Play catch. Combine cups and a small ball to create a catching game. Let the kids make the rules. What other games can you invent using the cups?

Notes

_____

_____

_____

_____

_____

_____

_____

Be a hero, check out the next chapter…

Hero Play

Overview

What is super hero play? It is a form of creative or pretend play in which children imitate action heroes that they admire. In a child's social and moral development, playing "good guys" versus "bad guys" is very normal and important for their growth.

—Daniel J. Hodgins, *Get Over It! Relearning Guidance Practices*

Dan's right. Hero play is a chance to learn about social cuing, body language, and self-regulation as well as to play with big concepts like *life, death, risk, power, control, leadership, heroism, grit, sacrifice,* and more. Hero play is also a valuable play pathway to building large and small muscles, learning about cause-and-effect relationships, problem solving, language skills....The list goes on and on.

The problem, of course, is that adults often see this type of play as too loud, too violent, too chaotic, and too rowdy for early learning settings. It is often discouraged, and it is sometimes banned.

Unless you are a girl.

The go-to "action heroes" for many little girls are moms and princesses. In the eyes of the children playing, these heroes are as powerful, smart, and daring as Batman and Captain America ("I'm the mom, and I said so! Clean your room!" and "You *have* to do what the princess says, and *I* am the princess!") These heroes are more socially acceptable in early learning settings because they are not as likely to climb the furniture, wrestle their foes to the ground, and yell about saving the day.

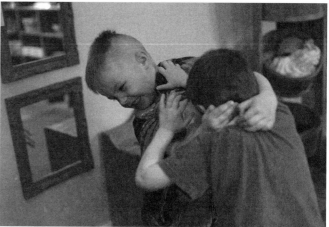

The result is that the quiet kids engaging in socially acceptable hero play reap the benefits, while the boys and girls who are drawn to rough, loud, and rambunctious hero play miss out.

Why It's Important

Children need safe play environments to practice social skills, toy with moral concepts, and try on emotions. For some children, that play environment is full of capes, robots, masks, villains, superpowers, and laser guns. These things become symbols for the concepts with which they are playing. For example, an imaginary laser rifle is more about *power*, *control*, and *leadership* than it is about violence. Supporting all kinds of hero play is important because it helps kids learn valuable concepts and skills that they will use throughout their lives.

How to Support It

1. Remember that it's just play. The violence, killing, aggression, threats, bravado, and all the rest are pretend, not real.

2. Set up your space—or at least a portion of it—to safely support hero play. For example, make it safe for kids to run, jump, flip, and pretend to fly.

3. Provide props or supplies children can use to create props for hero play.

4. Educate parents. Help them understand the value of such play.

Questions to Ask Yourself

1. What, if anything, gets under your skin about rowdy and wild hero play?

2. What kind of hero play did you engage in as a child? What did you learn from it?

3. If you are not ready for full-on superhero play in your program, what baby step can you take toward trusting children to engage in this type of play?

Notes

_____

_____

_____

_____

_____

_____

_____

Things get sticky in the next chapter…

Magnet Wall

Overview

Kids love magnets, and this project allows you to create a designated magnet play space that will hum with social interaction, problem solving, discovery, and child-led learning.

Ingredients

- [ ] a wooden fence
- [ ] oil drip pan
- [ ] 1½-inch wood screws
- [ ] 1¼-inch pan head screws
- [ ] drill, screwdriver bit, and ⅛-inch bit
- [ ] two 24-inch-long 1-by-4-inch boards
- [ ] level
- [ ] magnets

Let Them Learn around You, Not Because of You

Be aware of the learning that is occurring all around you, even when it is not occurring because of you. Open your eyes to child-led learning. Better yet, document it with pictures, videos, and notes. Recognize that children are competent enough to lead their own learning and that learning does not occur only when you, the adult, are "teaching." In fact, far more authentic and meaningful learning takes place when children make their own discoveries, solve their own problems, and seek answers to their own questions.

Process

1. Mount the two pieces of wood to the fence using the wood screws. Make sure the two pieces are mounted horizontally, spaced about 36 inches apart, level, and parallel to each other.

2. Use the ⅛-inch drill bit to make pilot holes in the drip pan, and then mount the drip pan vertically to the two boards using the pan head screws. Make sure the drip pan's lip faces inward, toward the fence, and that it's level.

3. Add magnets, and let the children play.

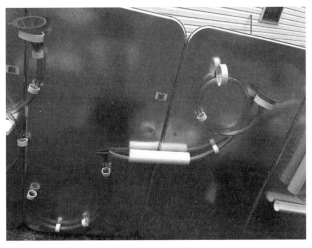

More Play Adventures

- Go horizontal. The above instructions explain how to mount the oil pan vertically. To mount it horizontally, use 36-inch-long boards, and mount them vertically, 24 inches apart, level, and parallel to each other.

- Go big. Use the instructions above to mount a series of oil drip pans and create a large magnet wall.

- Go mobile. On their own, oil drip pans are pretty flimsy and bend easily. To firm one up and create a mobile magnet wall, simply mount the pan to a piece of ¾-inch plywood slightly larger than the pan. Secure with ½-inch pan head screws. Then you can lean the mobile unit against a wall, place it on a tabletop, or even drill a few holes and hang it from the Suspended Branch of Play described in chapter 14.

- Go inside. For inside magnet-wall play, you can mount the drip pan directly to a wall. Make sure you screw into wall studs or use appropriate mounting anchors so that the pan is properly secured.

- Recycle. If you have access to old metal cookie sheets, muffin tins, or cake pans, you can mount them for use as mini magnet walls.

_____

_____

_____

_____

_____

_____

_____

_____

_____

_____

Don't be a fuddy or a duddy, go to the next chapter and get muddy…

Mud Kitchen

Overview

Kids love and learn from mud play, but because of the mess, it's play that doesn't happen often enough. That can change. Early learning programs can offer always-available mud play in their outside play areas by creating mud kitchens. Mud kitchens drip with preliteracy and prenumeracy learning, large- and small-muscle development, problem solving, and social skills practice. With a bit of thought and a bit of effort, you can create a mud kitchen that the children in your care (and you) will enjoy.

Ingredients

- ☐ child-height counter
- ☐ mixing basins
- ☐ water supply
- ☐ dirt supply
- ☐ mud play accessories: pots, pans, spoons, muffin tins, bowls, rolling pins, and so on

Process

1. Construct the mud play kitchen. Create one that has plenty of counter space, mixing basins (large plastic totes and old sinks work well), and mud play accessories. Situate it in a location with ready access to dirt and water.

2. Add storage. Hooks on fences and shelves under counters make it easy to put pots, pans, spoons, and trays away when it's time to clean up.

3. Establish program policies that will support regular mud play. For example, you could update your child dress code to ensure that kids arrive in mud-friendly clothing and footwear.

4. Let them make mud!

More Play Adventures

- Add textures. Make items like sand, pebbles, shells, sawdust, wood chips, straw, and flour available for kids to mix into their mud so they can create a variety of textures.

- Let the children design. Engage children in the design of the mud kitchen. Have discussions about where to locate the kitchen, how to set it up, and what it should include. Have them team up to draw pictures or build block mock-ups of the space they would like to create.

- Add scents. Providing fresh herbs, like mint, basil, and oregano, adds an olfactory element to mud play. You can also try providing things like vanilla or peppermint extract.

- Let the children collect. Get kids involved in collecting supplies for your mud kitchen. They can help make lists of needed items and take field trips to thrift shops and home centers to purchase supplies.

- Let the children set it up. Kids should also be involved in setting up the mud kitchen—this playful work is chock-full of social learning and problem solving.

- Let the children decide. Your mud kitchen will be a great space for all sorts of sensory play—with mud or without. Let the children come up with a menu of messy play concoctions. Then supply them with the ingredients they need. Or plop a variety of ingredients and see what they come up with!

Notes

_____

_____

_____

_____

_____

_____

_____

_____

_____

Flip the page, and please stay calm. In chapter 26 there's fizzing going on…

Fizzing Trail

Overview

In this exploration-rich activity, kids will have a chance to paint fizzy streaks of color onto the surface of a container full of vinegar. It's a chance to practice cooperation, problem solving, turn taking, sharing, and other social skills as well as a hands-on experience with color mixing, chemical reactions, and visual tracking.

Ingredients

- ☐ vinegar
- ☐ medium-sized shallow container (think small under-the-bed storage container)
- ☐ water
- ☐ baking soda
- ☐ liquid watercolor
- ☐ small cups or containers
- ☐ spoon
- ☐ paintbrushes

Process

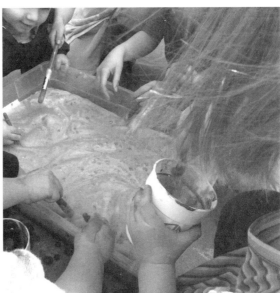

1. Pour 1 to 2 inches of vinegar into the shallow container.

2. To four or more small cups or containers, add baking soda, water, and a bit of liquid watercolor, and stir, creating a paste that has a cake-batter consistency. Go monochromatic and use the same color in each cup, or stir up a different color in each one.

3. Put paintbrushes into the cups of paste, and set them by the container of vinegar.

4. Step back, and let the children explore.

Note: To stretch your vinegar supply, you can dilute it with water at a 1:1 ratio. Also, the reaction works better if the paste in the cups is stirred regularly. You can let the kids discover this for themselves, or you can nudge them toward the discovery.

More Play Adventures

- Plop the paste. Mix a slightly thicker paste, roll it into small balls, and then drop the balls into the vinegar. You can even try creating multicolored paste balls.

- Spray the paste. Pour vinegar into a few small spray bottles. Paint different-colored pastes onto paper, sidewalks, brick walls, or other cleanable surfaces. Spray the paintings with the vinegar.

- Change the reaction. In step 1 above, add about ¼ cup of bubble solution to the vinegar. This will change the reaction when the paste is added.

- Color the vinegar. In step 1 above, add some liquid watercolor to the vinegar.

- Go very shallow. Try the activity with a ½ inch or less vinegar in the container. You may need to change out the vinegar once it becomes overrun with colored baking soda.

_____

_____

_____

_____

_____

_____

_____

Chapters aren't scarce; keep reading for a fresh one…

Planned Scarcity

Overview

A common practice in many early learning settings is to ensure that there are multiples of all the equipment so that conflict can be avoided. Eight kids, eight bottles of glue, and eight pairs of scissors make for a smooth and fight-free craft project. Six toddlers and a dozen baby dolls cut down on "*MINE!*"

Providing multiples of most everything has been standard operating procedure for so long, people just assume it is the best choice.

The idea of not having enough, of creating some scarcity, is seldom considered. We live in a consumer-driven world of plenty, after all, making the idea of not having enough of anything socially hard to stomach. Why not take this simple step to avoid conflict and make the day run smoother?

Why It's Important

Well, we have a few reasons.

First off, early learning should not be about making the day easier for caregivers as much as it should be about providing children with what they need *right here* and *right now* in *this* moment. (Note that we said *need*, not *want*.) Just because it makes the adult caregiver's day easier does not mean it is a good choice for children. For example, baby swings are overused in many programs because overstimulated infants fall asleep and sleeping babies are less demanding. These contraptions make the adult's day easier, but the baby would be better off on the floor with peers or in the arms of a tuned-in caregiver.

The main reason we encourage you to purposefully create some scarcity in your program is that it *can* create conflict. Conflict can be good once children get a bit older—say three and up—and are learning to autonomously navigate the social world. When there are not enough bottles of glue, kids are forced to practice sharing, waiting their turn, self-regulating, controlling their emotions, delaying gratification, problem solving, compromise, and so much more. Scarcity-induced conflict creates learning moments.

Learning all the skills mentioned in the previous paragraph is vital for survival in our world. We have to learn to wait our turn, compromise, share, and all the rest if we are going to be able to navigate the world as adults.

Eight bottles of glue for eight kids does not lead to these life lessons. Seven or six or five bottles of glue for eight kids does.

- -

Playful interaction allows a penalty-free rehearsal of the normal give-and-take necessary in social groups.

—Stuart Brown, MD, with Christopher Vaughan, *Play: How It Shapes the Brain, Opens the Imagination, and Invigorates the Soul*

- -

How to Support It

1. Purposefully create scarcity from time to time: not enough glue for everyone, a limited amount of tape, fewer paintbrushes.

2. Help children manage themselves. Kids who have never encountered "not enough for everyone" can have a hard time dealing with the concept. Kids who have never had to practice sharing can struggle with the concept. Be supportive and help them through the experience.

3. Expect some aggression. First-time sharing or turn waiting can sometimes lead to growls and threats. Expect them and be prepared to address them. (How you address it depends, of course, on the child and the situation. Strong emotional environments make managing these situations easier.)

Questions to Ask Yourself

1. How have you responded—as a child and as an adult—to scarcity, waiting your turn, and sharing?

2. How will you explain the need for planned scarcity to the children's parents?

3. How do you think each of the children in your care will respond to "not enough"?

Notes

_____

_____

_____

_____

_____

_____

_____

Turn the page for some frozen fun…

Frozen Sculptures

Overview

Children are amazed by the properties of water. Frozen water never ceases to amaze. This simple yet awe-inspiring and imagination-sparking activity uses the simplicity of frozen water in a novel way that sparks lots of conversations, interactions, and learning.

Ingredients

- [ ] plain white washcloths
- [ ] bucket of water
- [ ] cookie sheet
- [ ] freezer
- [ ] liquid watercolor
- [ ] cups
- [ ] paintbrushes

Process

1. Soak the washcloths in the bucket of water, remove them, and squeeze out a bit of water—but not too much.

2. Shape the washcloths: You can drape them over objects like water bottles or plastic dinosaurs, smooth them on a cookie sheet, or crumple them into balls. There's really no wrong way to do it.

3. Place the washcloths on the cookie sheet and put it into the freezer overnight.

4. Remove the washcloth sculptures from the freezer and let the children paint them with liquid watercolors that have been diluted with water.

5. Step back and observe the children's discoveries and imaginings as they play.

6. Rinse the washcloths when they are completely melted, and do the activity all over again.

More Play Adventures

- Connect them. Add rubber bands to the sculpture-making process so kids can connect washcloths together and make them hold their shape.

- Sculpt paper towels. Wet lots of paper towels, let kids crumple and shape them into sculptures, freeze them, and paint with colored water. Repeat as needed.

- Freeze playdough. Let kids create with playdough, freeze their creations overnight, and then play with the frozen dough the next day.

- Freeze mud. Make mud sculptures and freeze them; then return the sculptures to the mud play area for some frozen mud play.

- Freeze toys. Select a bunch of smallish plastic toys (cars, dinosaurs, blocks), place them in a cake pan full of water, and freeze. Add this giant ice cube to a tub of water, plop it on a table with a few towels, or drop it into the sandbox.

Notes

_____

_____

_____

_____

_____

_____

_____

Do the next chapter to support failure...

Support Failure

Overview

Learning to fail graciously is a valuable social skill. We've all met children—and adults—who have not developed this skill. They can be…challenging. All children should be willing to put in some effort, show some grit, and strive to succeed, but when they do not win the game or meet the challenge, they should be able to display some self-control, diplomacy, and elegance in their failure.

Learning to take an informed risk that may result in failure is even more valuable. Our factory-model education system has created learning environments where having the answer the teacher is looking for is more important than everything else. In this environment, many children choose not to offer any answers at all because the humiliation of offering up a wrong answer is too great to bear. This means they do not try, do not challenge themselves, and do not take learning risks. (The book *NurtureShock* has a chapter with more on this topic.)

We encourage you, as a caregiver, to create an environment that supports children's failure, a space where they can take learning risks and know they will not be shunned, looked down on, belittled, or admonished when they make a mistake.

Let Them Fail

Stop coming to the rescue every time you see a child heading toward failure. We all know that some of life's greatest lessons are learned through failure, yet we prevent young children from failing all the time. For a child to understand the value of perseverance and determination, failing is paramount. Failing can lead not only to new discoveries but also to learning determination, perseverance, and patience. Failing can be surprisingly empowering.

Let's face it. Failing happens in life a lot. Learning how to handle failure is a lifelong skill that young children deserve to practice.

Why It's Important

Failure does not enter the mind of an infant learning to walk or talk. She plunges headfirst into these tasks and rolls with the experience—learning from both her success and her failure. In our society, as children get older, they become keenly aware that failure is a bad thing. They stop taking risks, challenging themselves, and engaging in activities that could result in failure. This fear of failure cuts out lots of learning opportunities for lots of children.

By making failure okay—and even supporting it—we help kids become more resilient, robust, and ready to take on the unknowns life is always offering up.

How to Support It

1. Let kids see you fail and make mistakes. Let them see you shrug these things off and move on. Show them that a mistake or error does not bring the world to a screeching halt.

2. Have one-on-one conversations about mistakes and failure. Discuss how these things make you feel.

3. Don't jump on kids that mess up. Spilt milk is spilt milk. It's easy to clean it up and to move on to other things.

4. When a child takes a calculated risk that results in failure, ask him, "What did you learn?" and have a discussion about what just happened.

Questions to Ask Yourself

1. Have you ever been scared to take a risk or put yourself on the spot because you were afraid of failure? How did it feel? Why did you feel this way?

2. What valuable life lessons have you learned by making a mistake?

3. What two baby steps can you take to make your learning environment more failure friendly?

Notes

_____

_____

_____

_____

_____

_____

_____

Turn off the lights. Proceed to the next chapter…

Flashlight Bling with Some Cling

Overview

This activity combines two things children love—flashlights and magnets. Flashlight Bling with Some Cling offers children ample opportunities to lead play, explore, and learn socially. It will build their understanding of physical science topics like light and shadows, magnetic attraction and repulsion, and ferrous and nonferrous metals. Oh, and along the way they'll have a chance to hone hand-eye coordination, visual tracking, and cause-and-effect thinking skills.

Ingredients

☐ flashlights

☐ magnets (magnetic hematite is recommended, but ceramic magnets will work fine)

☐ hot glue gun

☐ metal bits: paper clips, screws, washers, and the like

Process

1. Secure the magnets around the lens of each flashlight using hot glue. Allow the glue to cool and dry completely.

2. Turn off the lights.

3. Plop the flashlights and the metal bits, and let the play unfold.

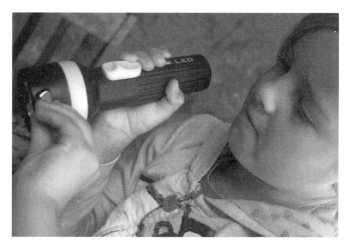

More Play Adventures

- Attach a magnet to a piece of ½-inch dowel with colored duct tape to create a magic wand that can pick up paper clips, screws, and washers.

- Use duct tape to secure a small LED flashlight to a pair of plastic tongs and give kids small items to manipulate.

- Another paintbrush idea: duct-tape a number of paintbrushes around the lens of a flashlight, turn out the lights, and let the kids paint.

- Yet another painting idea: duct-tape a small paint roller to a flashlight, kill the lights, and paint.

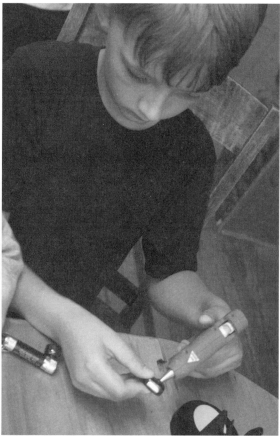

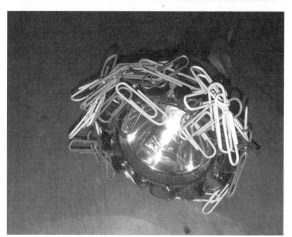

Notes

_____

_____

_____

_____

_____

_____

_____

Want to play with a BSO? Continue on to the next chapter and give it a go…

Sticky Side Out

Overview

Children are fascinated with tape, and that fascination leads to learning if it's given half a chance. Sticky-side-out tape is a BSO that spurs interaction, conversation, contemplation, and exploration—all of which lead to learning.

Ingredients

- ☐ rolls of 2-inch masking tape
- ☐ assorted small odds and ends: scrap paper, glitter, Cheerios, paper clips, craft pom-poms, and so on

Process

1. Loosely wrap children's hands with masking tape, sticky side out. Let them decide if they want their thumbs to be free or wrapped up in the tape. Let them choose whether they want both hands wrapped or just one.

2. Allow the children to play at picking up the bits and pieces you've plopped with their sticky hands.

3. Follow the children's lead as their play evolves.

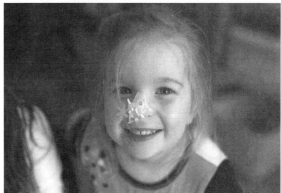

The push for achievement in all quantifiable realms, especially the academic, begins so early that preschools all around the country are focusing less and less on the development of social skills and self-regulation and more and more on academics. However, children of that age are so unready for curricular focus that preschools report a rising tide of behavioral problems—and wind up expelling six out of every thousand students. Imagine: expelled from preschool! With so much expected of them when they have not yet mastered socialization and self-regulation—two skills that are intricately interconnected and both of which foster academic excellence—more of them are acting out. Expectations for children have gone completely haywire, untethered from any reference to children's developmental needs, referenced only to deep adult anxieties.

—**Hara Estroff Marano,** *A Nation of Wimps:*
The High Cost of Invasive Parenting

More Play Adventures

- Other sticky parts. Move beyond the children's hands, and wrap whole arms, legs, and torsos with sticky-side-out tape. How about creating sticky-side-out mummies? Note that avoiding wrapping heads in tape is a good idea because it avoids pulling out hair and suffocation. Kids with long hair might want to tuck it into a hat before doing a whole-body wrap.

- Sticky things. Wrap objects like blocks, balls, and stuffed frogs in sticky-side-out tape, and then step back to see what kind of play unfolds.

- Sticky collages. Wrap hunks of cardboard, cookie sheets, and pizza pans with sticky-side-out tape, and then let kids use small bits of construction paper, wrapping paper, aluminum foil, and the like to create collages.

Notes

_____

_____

_____

_____

_____

_____

_____

Save the drama for your mama in the next chapter…

Dramatic Play

Overview

When it comes to developing and practicing social skills, nothing beats dramatic play. Whether kids are playing house or superheroes, the learning is rich and varied. Dramatic play gives children a chance to practice the give-and-take of relationships, work on self-regulation, and sort and classify the world. It is also an opportunity to safely play with real-world scenarios and make sense of them. Parental arguments, things seen on television, overheard bits of adult conversation, trips to the grocery store, and everything else that grabs a child's attention can find its way into dramatic play, where the child can turn it inside out and try to make sense of it.

Yet, in our rush-through-childhood-to-high-pressure/high-stakes-testing world, dramatic play is disappearing. Space for such play is vanishing in many kindergarten classrooms. It is even dying off in some preschool settings.

We want you to consider treating dramatic play like it's an endangered species and do everything you can to promote it, protect it, and help it thrive.

Why It's Important

Dramatic play offers children a safe haven for exploring their feelings, thoughts, knowledge, and experiences. Without large blocks of time for such play, children miss out on the dynamic real-time social learning dramatic play has to offer.

How to Support It

1. Make your dramatic play area as flexible as possible. In most programs, this space gets set up like a kitchen and stays that way. Kitchen play is fine, but a more flexible space will lead to a wider variety of play.

2. Let the children own the space. Avoid deciding for the children when the space needs to change and how. Give these decisions over to the children, and then do all you can to support their interests and needs.

3. Remember to say "Yes…And" (see chapter 19).

4. Provide plenty of loose parts (see chapter 6).

5. Make plenty of time for children's dramatic play to develop and unfold. It takes time for kids to come up with a scenario, collect props, select roles, and get the play started.

6. Remember that dramatic play happens in other areas and look for ways to support it. For example, keeping a zoo of plastic animals near the block area increases the likelihood that dramatic play will unfold in this space.

7. Remember that superhero play, rough-and-tumble play, death play, monster play, and war play are all forms of dramatic play and need to be supported. Remember also that play is in the child, not in the toy—and some kids *need* to let this type of play out.

Questions to Ask Yourself

1. What are your dramatic play memories?

2. What small step can you take this week to better support dramatic play?

3. What types of dramatic play do you shut down? Why?

Notes

_____

_____

_____

_____

_____

_____

_____

Keep reading for some saturation experimentation...

Saturation Experimentation

Overview

Child-led play, exploration, and discovery allow children ownership of their learning. Such play, exploration, and discovery are also the prime time to practice social skills. This simple activity—applying colored water to a leak-resistant drop cloth—is a gateway to cooperation, problem solving, conversation, self-regulation, and more.

Ingredients

- [ ] any disposable drop cloth with an absorbent top layer and a leak-resistant bottom layer
- [ ] liquid watercolor
- [ ] cups
- [ ] straws and/or pipettes
- [ ] water

Process

1. To avoid drips, cut the drop cloth a bit smaller than the table you're going to place it on.

2. Mix up four or more cups of colored water using the liquid watercolor.

3. Spread the drop cloth onto the table. Plop the cups of colored water and the straws and/or pipettes on top of it.

4. Let the children engage with the materials. Be available for support.

More Play Adventures

- Make prints. After the drop cloth is fully saturated with colored water, provide some paper towels. If you'd like, you can demonstrate how to make a print by pressing the flat paper towel onto the drop cloth. Or you can simply step back to see if the kids make this discovery for themselves.

- Print another day. Let the drop cloth dry completely and then store it away for another day. When you want to print again, rewet the drop cloth with clean water using paintbrushes or pipettes, and print away. You can also squirt the drop cloth with more colored water, if you'd like.

- Go vertical. Hang the drop cloth on a wall or fence. Allow the children to apply color with paintbrushes or spray bottles.

- Recycle the drop cloth, part I. The drop cloth cannot be washed, but it can be reused. Let it dry out completely, and store it for next time—or let the children cut it up for arts and crafts projects.

- Recycle the drop cloth, part II. Let the drop cloth dry completely and allow children to use it for building forts or other dramatic play.

Let Them Have Freedom of Time

Evaluate your schedule. A quality early learning program does not need to divide its day into fifteen different segments. A quality early learning program should have a flexible schedule that allows children to lead learning, solve problems, and own failures. There should be time for children to make choices, assess risk, and handle conflict. And there should be time for children to get into deep play where authentic, meaningful learning occurs and they are empowered by trust and control.

Denita Has an Idea II

During an evening of drinking wine and launching peanut butter, ketchup, pickles, mustard, baking soda, colored vinegar, paint, whiskey, shaving cream, and other stuff at a drop cloth hanging in Jeff's studio with him and early learning play goddess Lisa "the Ooey Gooey Lady" Murphy, I could not stop thinking about the absorption capabilities of the drop cloth. The fact that it was lined with plastic made it beyond awesome because it was so mess resistant. Not a drop of the mess made it onto Jeff's oak floor.

The next day my brain was still stuck on the awesomeness of that drop cloth. I was determined to find a way for my littles to have fun with it. I went to Walmart, purchased a 10-by-12-foot drop cloth for right around six dollars, and eagerly awaited Monday morning.

I plopped the drop cloth on the table, and set the cups of colored water and pipettes right on top of it. The children dove in headfirst, and it didn't take long for the conversations to emerge and the collaboration to occur. "Hey, Gavin, you squirt the yellow, and I'll squirt the blue. Let's make green!" The tarp became a masterpiece even the most faithful 1970s flower child would envy. To milk the process (that is, to make the supplies last longer and to keep the children's interest alive) once all the colored water had been squirted onto the drop cloth, I quickly tore off pieces of paper towel and placed them onto the saturated drop cloth. With just one finger, I gently pressed a paper towel. The bright color from the drop cloth instantly came through onto the paper towel. The children loved this! Soon, one finger at a time, they were joining in on the colorful fun.

And then the game changer happened. Jack took *both* hands and laid them on a piece of paper towel at the same time. He lifted them and revealed rainbow handprints. A "WOW!" escaped him, his face full of amazement and his eyes sparkling with the awareness of the possibilities. The children reacted to Jack's discovery in a way that made me so proud. They scoured the room for objects to make their own prints with, not content to do exactly what Jack had done. They pressed lids, plastic plates, blocks, and dinosaur feet onto the white paper towel and were amazed by each print they made. They even drove cars across the paper towels, leaving rainbow tracks in their paths.

You can see video from the evening with Jeff and Lisa that sparked this activity idea here: www.youtube.com/watch?v=Pac8z3n8m_M&feature= share&list=UUSA4zKk4FyiKGzdtLFLO9gw and here: www.youtube.com/watch?v=K-3cdaDkdAI&feature=share&list=UUSA4zKk4FyiKGzdtLFLO9gw.

Notes

_____

_____

_____

_____

_____

_____

_____

Problem: This chapter is over. Solution: Turn the page…

34 Problem Solving

Overview

Once upon a time, adults had to spend a lot of time ensuring that families had basic necessities like food and shelter. Back then, kids spent most of their time in mixed-age groups of peers, leading their own learning and solving their own problems as they played and explored.

Now it seems like there is always a well-intentioned adult hovering nearby, ready to swoop in and solve problems as they happen—or, just as likely, to clear a problem-free path for children to stroll down. If she's not leaping in to stop Timmy from hitting Tina because he has *that look* on his face when Tina chooses not to share the markers, then she's keeping him away from Tina entirely because he is a bad influence or too aggressive. Helicopter and snowplow adults mean well, but their efforts steal from children's opportunities to struggle, think, act, and solve problems on their own. This means children have few real-life opportunities to practice problem solving.

We encourage you to swim against the tide and let kids solve their own problems whenever possible—when in doubt, let them work it out.

Why It's Important

While stopping the conflict between Timmy and Tina may seem like the responsible thing to do—it keeps Tina from getting hit after all—it steals a learning opportunity from both children. Timmy misses out on the chance to choose a different course of action, and just because he has a reputation as a hitter does not mean he is always going to be the kid who hits. He misses the chance to solve the problem by waiting his turn to use the markers or choosing to use the crayons instead. And, if he chooses to hit, stopping it before it happens takes away his opportunity to experience the consequences of hitting—Tina's tears, the adult's disapproval, and so on.

Tina loses out too. She misses a chance to negotiate with Timmy ("I'll be done with the markers as soon as I color in this space monster. Then you can have them," or "I only need green—you can have the rest of them."). She also misses the chance to practice some resiliency and assertiveness ("NO, Timmy! It's not polite to hit people! I don't like that!").

Practice in the real-world ebb and flow of relationships is the only way we humans get good at solving interpersonal and other problems. Taking away children's chances to practice solving problems steals their opportunity to learn skills they will use their whole lives.

How to Support It

1. Step back a bit. If you have to hover, do it from a bit farther away. Be close enough to stop any real danger or injury, but as much as you can, let kids have enough space to engage in and manage their own problems.

2. Create a healthy emotional environment. Kids who feel safe, secure, loved, trusted, and valued are better equipped to handle problems that need solving.

3. Create problems. Once in a while you can set up problems for children to solve. For example, let them hunt down a "lost" pair of shoes or

move a heavy table. This gives them a chance to strategize and work as a team to rectify the problem.

4. Inform parents. Discuss with parents the value in letting children solve child-sized problems, and support them in getting on board with the idea. Help them realize that when children solve small problems today, they are better prepared for solving adult-sized problems later in life.

Questions to Ask Yourself

1. How did you feel as a child when someone swooped in and solved a problem you were capable of handling?

2. How often do you hover or plow paths for the children in your care?

3. What one small step could you take to better support children as problem solvers?

Notes

_____

_____

_____

_____

_____

_____

_____

In the next chapter you'll clap for clips…

Chip Clips

Overview

Plopping a bunch of chip clips into your early learning space is a fun way to spark exploration and discovery among a group of kids. Plus, opening and closing the clips is a great way for the younger ones to build the small-muscle strength and control necessary for manipulating a pencil when they get a bit older. This kind of play also hones hand-eye coordination—another preliteracy skill.

- -

Social relationships, it turns out, have deep evolutionary roots. You will not escape the need in your lifetime.

—**John Medina**, *Brain Rules for Baby:*
How to Raise a Smart and Happy Child from Zero to Five

- -

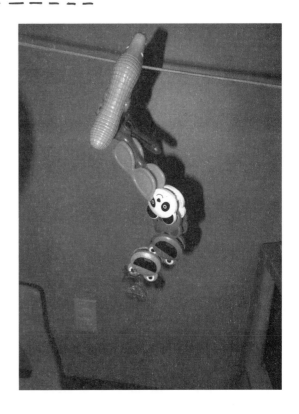

Ingredients

- ☐ various chip clips. Once you start looking for them, you'll find them all over the place in all kinds of fun shapes and colors.
- ☐ ⅛-inch nylon rope

Process

1. At an angle, secure a piece of rope across the room so that the clips will freely slide from the high end to the low end of the rope. Secure the high end of the rope high enough that the kids will have to stand on a stable chair or platform to reach it. (Remember, this kind of managed risk taking helps children build confidence and learn to assess danger.)

2. Plop the clips. If the clips are brand-new, let the children figure out how to unpackage them.

3. Step back and observe the play. It's possible your crew won't think to hang the clips on the rope at first—and that's okay. That's the beauty of child-led play. Follow their lead.

More Play Adventures

1. Clip a pendulum. Secure one end of the rope from the ceiling so that the loose end dangles a few inches above the floor. Let the kids add clips to the rope and swing it. As play progresses, they'll likely discover they can use the clips to attach objects like baby blankets, dolls, and pieces of paper to the rope. Follow the children's lead and see where the exploration takes you.

2. Be a hero. Gather clips and some old towels or baby blankets. Secure superhero capes to kids using the clips. Since the clips do not have a lot of clamping power, they readily release if someone pulls on Super-man's cape or if Batman gets hung up on a piece of furniture.

3. Do clip painting. You can make DIY paintbrushes by securing bits of sponge, fabric, shower puffs, dried grass blades, ribbon, or rope in the jaws of a clip. Tape the jaws shut if you want the items to better stay in place.

4. Give them a home. Giving clips a regular home in your play space will lead to all kinds of inventive play. Just find a logical and accessible place for them to live in your space, and let kids know where to find them.

Notes

_____

_____

_____

_____

_____

_____

_____

You'll get mixed up in the next chapter…

Mix It Up

Overview

There are a lot of great recipes out in the world for playdough, paint, and sensory play concoctions, but for kids, the process of creating the concoctions is just as learning rich as play with the finished product. Mixing it up is half the fun. All the scooping, stirring, measuring, mixing, kneading, and the like leads kids to preliteracy and prenumeracy learning, problem solving, and small-muscle development. When they mix up recipes in groups, they get real-world, real-time social skills practice.

Ingredients

- ☐ bowls
- ☐ spoons
- ☐ measuring cups

- ☐ ingredients (Use your imagination: water, flour, dirt, food coloring, ice, sand, oatmeal, glitter, and so on.)

- ☐ hand-washing bucket, washcloths, and towels

Process

1. Plop the materials in a mess-friendly location.

2. Step back and let the children mix it up, and then follow their lead. Support their play with materials and assistance as needed.

More Play Adventures

- Promote repeatability. Suggest kids keep track of how much of *this* and *that* they add to their random mixtures so they will be able to re-create the mixture if they come up with something really neat. Help them name and record their recipes. You could even create your own classroom play-concoction recipe book.

- Encourage variations on a theme. Start out with a few components (water and coffee grounds, for example) in a large container, and then see how many different concoctions the children can mix up in smaller containers from that base.

- Follow recipes. All those recipes we mentioned in the chapter overview? Collect some from books, Pinterest, and other places and then let the kids mix them up. Help as much as is needed—but no more.

- Hit the kitchen. Why not get children involved in mixing up edibles in the kitchen? It's a great offshoot of the above activities. Plus, kids will feel really empowered, trusted, respected, and valued when they get to make things for their playmates to eat.

Notes

_____

_____

_____

_____

_____

_____

_____

Don't sit here waiting, turn the page for some gravity painting…

Dribble Painting

Overview

Dribble painting is another deceptively simple activity that will lead to social interaction, conversation, experimentation, and learning—and all you're doing is allowing kids to drip runny paint down a paper ramp.

The lack of unstructured play for youngsters is associated with less enthusiasm for learning, diminished creativity, and poorer social skills.

—Madeline Levine, *Teach Your Children Well: Why Values and Coping Skills Matter More than Grades, Trophies, or "Fat Envelopes"*

Ingredients

- ☐ butcher paper
- ☐ tape
- ☐ paint
- ☐ water
- ☐ paint cups
- ☐ paintbrushes

Process

1. Find a messy-play safe location and use tape and a sheet of butcher paper about 6 feet long to create a ramp. (This is something you probably shouldn't do around your new tan suede sofa and white carpet.)

2. Squirt some paint into a paint cup and add water to dilute it. You're looking for a nice runny consistency.

3. Use the paintbrushes to dribble the paint onto the upper edge of the paper ramp. Then step back and see what kind of play the kids bring to the materials.

More Play Adventures

- Use spray bottles. Apply color to the ramp with spray bottles.

- Guide it. Blow through drinking straws to guide the dribbles of paint down the paper ramp.

- Get in the gutter. Use a section of plastic rain gutter as a ramp. Because the pigment will not soak into the plastic, colors will mix as they move down the ramp.

- Adjust the grade. Play with the angle of your ramp: Steep ramps equal fast dribbles. Small inclines equal slow-moving dribbles.

- Dribble paint up the ramp. Plop some color at the bottom of the ramp and see if kids can use drinking straws, a blow-dryer (set on cool), or a fan to make the paint go up.

- Blow it up. While you have the blow-dryer out, why not try using cool air to push other objects up the paper ramp? Try things like bits of yarn, cotton balls, feathers, and aluminum-foil balls. The balloon pumps from chapter 13 work great for this variation too.

- Paint balls. Shake marbles or small balls in some paint, and then roll them down a paper ramp.

- Get dramatic. Set up a ramp in your dramatic play space, step back, and see how the kids choose to use it.

Notes

_____

_____

_____

_____

_____

_____

_____

Turning to the next chapter is not a big project. Give it a try…

Projects

Overview

Back in the day, kids had the time and trust to take on all kinds of projects: things like constructing tree houses, digging holes, building go-carts, saving cats stuck in trees, hunting for four-leaf clovers, and damming streams. These projects led to lots of social interaction and learning. Kids made decisions, solved problems, overcame obstacles, organized materials, and stretched muscles. They negotiated, struggled, toiled, strained, persevered, failed, and succeeded.

Today, because their days are so often controlled by adults, children do not have as much opportunity to take on projects as freely as their parents and grandparents once did. We encourage you to bring projects back into the lives of children.

Why It's Important

Taking on their own projects gives children—as individuals and in groups—the chance to own their learning. It is a chance for them to be in control, to lead, and to learn through experiences. It is also an opportunity for them to have an idea, take some initiative, and then follow through on the idea. This is great practice for adulthood. A child who conceives of an idea, like a go-cart, and is then able to work freely at bringing the idea from her imagination into the physical world is an empowered child. Too often, kids are restrained from pursing their imaginings. When they hear *no* and *can't* and *don't* too often, they give up, become reluctant to voice their ideas, and even become fearful of taking on new challenges.

How to Support It

1. Provide plenty of time and trust so kids feel free to take on projects as they pop into their busy brains.

2. Make appropriate materials available as children start working on projects. Sometimes kids may need your help hunting down specific materials for a project. Other times they will be able to work with readily available open-ended materials already in your play space. Stay tuned in and ready to help them as needed.

3. Support their efforts just enough. Too much support will make them feel you have taken over.

4. Read up on the Project Approach. We recommend starting here: www .projectapproach.org.

Questions to Ask Yourself

1. What projects did you take on as a child?

2. How did you feel when you were allowed to take on a project and succeed or fail on your own?

3. How much adult support did you want as a child when you were working on a project?

4. As a child, what kinds of social skills did you get a chance to practice when working on projects with other children?

5. What changes could you make to your play space to better support child-led projects?

Notes

_____

_____

_____

_____

_____

_____

_____

Flip to the next chapter and see that sometimes one handle is not enough...

Double-Handled Paintbrushes

Overview

These DIY double-handled paintbrushes are a fun way for pairs of children to cooperate on art projects. They are sure to lead to lots of conversation, problem solving, and social skills practice as kids work to manipulate and create with them.

- -

A child who begins kindergarten knowing letters and sounds may be cognitively prepared, but if he or she does not understand how to listen, share, take turns, and get along with teachers and classmates, this lack of socialization will hinder further learning.

—Dorothy G. Singer, Roberta Michnick Golinkoff, and Kathy Hirsh-Pasek, *Play = Learning: How Play Motivates and Enhances Children's Cognitive and Social-Emotional Growth*

- -

Ingredients

- ☐ two wooden dowels about 18 inches long
- ☐ fabric scraps
- ☐ duct tape
- ☐ paint
- ☐ paper
- ☐ paper plate

Process

1. Cut the fabric scraps into strips 12 inches to 18 inches long.

2. Stack the scraps in a fairly neat pile.

3. Tape a dowel securely to each end of the stack of scraps.

4. Bring the handles together to form a U shape, and then tightly wrap a strip of duct tape around the fabric about 1½ inches above the dowels. The result will be a pair of dowels adhered to a closed loop of fabric strips.

5. Fluff the fabric a bit so the strips are not so neatly stacked.

6. Provide paper (hang it on an easel, tape it to a wall, put it on the floor, or place it on a table).

7. Squirt some paint onto a paper plate.

8. Step back and let pairs of children work the paintbrush together.

More Play Adventures

- Try different materials. For handles, try things like chopsticks, sticks, rope, or plastic tubing. For brush tips, try rubber bands, string, leather, bubble wrap, sponges, drinking straws, plastic wrap, or long blades of grass from your yard.

- The more, the merrier. Can you design and build a paintbrush that three or more kids can use together?

- Build paintbrushes with handles of various lengths. Painting with a brush that has a 3-foot-long handle is a different experience than using one with a 3-inch-long handle.

- Experiment with different ways to use the brushes. Which way gets the most interesting results? For example, do certain brushes work best if you dab the paint instead of applying it with long strokes? Are some brushes better for splatting and sprinkling paint?

- Vary the canvas location. Keep play with your DIY brushes fresh by changing up the location and position of the surface you are painting. Instead of a tabletop, try placing your canvas on the floor, on a wall, taped to the bottom of a table, or even hanging by rope from a tree branch.

Notes

Read on, and reward yourself with the next chapter…

Rewards

Overview

It has become common practice for adults to use carrots and sticks, rewards and punishments, to persuade, cajole, entice, nudge, and coax children into compliance. ("Clean your room and you can have thirty minutes on the Xbox." "Poop in the potty and you can put a sticker on the chart." "Make Mommy happy and eat your green beans.") The problem with these inducements is that, as Alfie Kohn writes in *Punished by Rewards: The Trouble with Gold Stars, Incentive Plans, A's, Praise, and Other Bribes*, "When we are repeatedly offered extrinsic motivators, we come to find the task or behavior for which we are rewarded less appealing in itself than we did before (or than other people do). Thereafter, our intrinsic motivation having shrunk, we are less likely to engage in the activity unless offered an inducement for doing so. After a while, we appear to be responsive to—indeed, to require—rewards. But it is the prior use of rewards that made us that way!"

It's a vicious cycle. Rewards lead to a desire for more rewards, and intrinsic motivation is replaced by a desire—a need—for extrinsic confirmation of personal value and worth. Children grow dependent on stickers, praise, and treats.

We would like you to push back against the rewards culture that exists in many early learning settings and support children as they develop their internal locus of control and intrinsic motivation.

Why It's Important

Trying to motivate children with rewards can actually kill off their motivation—and worse.

When children grow dependent on the rewards the adults in their lives dole out, it becomes more and more difficult for them to self-motivate. The rewards culture can also lead children to stop trying new things, stop putting in effort, and other negative things. In *Drive: The Surprising Truth about What Motivates Us*, Daniel H. Pink writes, "Carrots and sticks can achieve precisely the opposite of their intended aims. Mechanisms designed to increase motivation can dampen it. Tactics aimed at boosting creativity can reduce it. Programs to promote good deeds

can make them disappear. Meanwhile, instead of restraining negative behavior, rewards and punishments can often set it loose—and give rise to cheating, addiction, and dangerously myopic thinking."

How to Support It

1. Be mindful of your use of rewards. Try keeping a tally sheet of how many times you offer up different rewards in the course of a day.

2. Stop using stickers, praise, and other rewards for actions and behaviors you feel are simply appropriate for the children to be doing. Stopping all at once may be tough, so take baby steps. Wean yourself from using rewards over time.

3. Support children as they work—and sometimes struggle—to develop self-control. Learning to self-govern is a process that requires time and practice.

4. Help children see the natural rewards for their choices and actions. For example: "Now that you have cleaned up the play area, it will be much easier to find the toys you need." "How does it feel to put on your shoes all by yourself?"

5. Read up on rewards. We recommend Kohn's book *Punished by Rewards* and *NurtureShock* by Po Bronson and Ashley Merryman.

Questions to Ask Yourself

1. Have you ever found yourself overly dependent on praise, rewards, and the approval of others?

2. When has intrinsic motivation helped you meet a goal or overcome an obstacle?

3. What kinds of rewards do you offer up, whom do you offer them to, and why?

4. How can you educate parents about the importance of intrinsic motivation?

Notes

_____

_____

_____

_____

_____

_____

_____

Turn to the next chapter for some conclusions…

Conclusion

We hope the preceding pages sparked some ideas and encouraged you to take a few baby steps toward learning environments that are more child-led, play-full, and open-ended. While we believe books are useful containers for sharing ideas and offering support, we do not believe our job as authors ends when you put down your highlighter and close up the pages. Too often, people read books like this one, get inspired to *try a new thing* or to *make some sort of change,* when real life takes over and forces the new thing or the change to the sideline. We feel our job—*after book*—is to be a continuing source of support. So, if you have questions, require inspiration, want to share stories, pictures, or ideas, need a hand to hold while you take a baby step, or just want to connect, here is how you can find us:

We both pay attention to the Let Them Play Facebook page: www.facebook.com/letthemplaybook.

And you can connect to us individually online with these links:

Denita
playcounts.denitadinger@gmail.com
www.playcounts.com
http://playcountsdenitadinger.blogspot.com
www.facebook.com/pages/Play-Counts/141352815884541

Jeff
jeffajohnson@cableone.net
www.explorationsearlylearning.com
www.facebook.com/explorationsearlylearning
www.youtube.com/user/ExplorationsLLC
www.pinterest.com/exearlylearning

Social Play Terminology

The following is an incomplete but useful list of skills, types of play, and other terms related to social play.

adaptability: This is the ability to go with the flow—to change or be changed to fit current circumstances.

altruism: This is the unselfish concern for the well-being of others.

associative play: This is when children play together with similar toys but without organization, direction, or goals.

collaboration: This is the ability to work with one or more people to complete a task. The ability to collaborate requires social skills such as nonverbal communication, adaptability, and empathy. Children hone collaboration skills when they play games, engage in dramatic play, and work on projects.

compromising: This is when an agreement or settlement of a dispute is reached by each side making a concession.

conflict-resolution skills: These are social, personal, and thinking skills used to resolve disagreements and differences with others. Building these skills and using them effectively takes time and practice. There is also a lot of trial and error involved, because children must learn which conflict-resolution skills are socially acceptable. For example, punching a peer may end a conflict, but it is not as socially acceptable as verbal negotiation.

conscientiousness: This means being governed by conscience, being principled, and being mindful of other people's needs and desires.

contribution: This is the act of giving to the greater social community. Contributing may take an active form, like pitching in to help clean up after a meal, or it may be something passive, like choosing not to pull your sister's hair while Dad is navigating the minivan across three lanes of traffic to exit the freeway and get to the waterslide.

conversational skills: These are the skills needed to communicate in person with others. Conversation skills include using and reading body language, making appropriate eye contact, paying attention, asking and answering questions, and listening. Developing these skills takes a lot of real-world practice.

cooperation: Cooperation is the process of working with others to achieve an agreed-upon end.

cooperative play: This is group play organized around a specific purpose, goal, dramatization, or formal game.

delayed gratification: Gratification that is put off until time has passed, a task has been completed, an obstacle has been overcome, or some other criterion has been met. The ability to delay gratification is an important self-governance skill.

empathy: This is the ability to understand or be sensitive to the feelings of others—the capacity to see things from another person's perspective. This skill develops over time as children move from a "me"-centric view of the world to a worldview that considers the feelings of others.

executive function: This refers to the role of the brain in organizing information, controlling impulses, learning from mistakes, assessing risks, and keeping an eye on the big picture.

eye contact: Making good eye contact is tough. Too much eye contact and you come across as too intense or as a creepy gawker. Too little eye contact and other people might think you don't care about what they have to say. It takes practice to find the right balance.

fantasy play: This is make-believe play.

grit: This means courage and resolve, strength of character, and determination. Having grit means being able to persist in challenging circumstances.

honesty: This is the quality of being fair and truthful with others.

initiating interactions: This is the ability to start an interpersonal exchange. It requires social skills such as the ability to read body language, start a conversation, feel and show empathy, overcome fear, and the like.

leadership: This is being able to persuade, direct, and encourage others to follow a particular course of action.

listening skills: Listening skills allow us to hear with understanding by receiving auditory information, attending to it, processing it, and responding to it. Listening skills include making eye contact, managing body language, asking questions, showing empathy, and concentrating on what the speaker is saying.

loyalty: This is a feeling of strong support for someone or something.

mindfulness: This is being conscious or aware of one's surroundings and interactions with those surroundings.

nonverbal communication: This is the process of sending and receiving information through gestures, posture, facial expressions, eye movement, and touch. Children practice these skills during dramatic play, outside play, small-group time, meals, and one-on-one time with the adult caregiver and other children.

onlooker behavior: This is when a child mostly watches other children play.

parallel play: This is when a child plays independently with toys that are similar to those being used by nearby children but with no effort to engage the nearby children.

patience: This is the ability to peacefully accept delay. Children learn this when they take turns at the drinking fountain, when they wait for their turn while playing Candy Land, and when they watch the calendar waiting for the day they can celebrate their birthday.

perseverance: This is steadfastness in doing something despite difficulty or delay in achieving success.

persistence: Persistence is the quality that allows someone to continue doing something or trying to do something even though it is difficult or opposed by others.

personal space: This is the region surrounding a person that he regards as psychologically his own.

persuasion: Persuasion is causing people to do or to believe something.

respect: Respect is the feeling of deep admiration for someone or something.

self-calming: This is the ability to self-regulate by reigning in anger, fear, and other strong emotions to restore personal equilibrium.

self-confidence: This is faith in one's abilities, qualities, and judgment.

self-governance/self-regulation/self-control: These are the abilities to manage one's emotions and actions, including the ability to delay gratification.

sense of community: This is a feeling of belonging or inclusion, of being part of a group, or of fitting in with a peer group.

sharing: Sharing is the joint use of a material or space.

sociodramatic play: This is the most advanced form of social and symbolic play. In this type of play, children carry out imitation, drama, symbolic play, and fantasy play.

solitary play: This is when a child plays independently with toys that are different from those being used by nearby children and with no effort to engage the nearby children.

symbolic play: Symbolic play is dramatic play that occurs when children begin to substitute one object for another, for example, using a hairbrush as a microphone when playing rock star.

Suggested Reading

Adventure: The Value of Risk in Children's Play, by Joan Almon

Are We Scaring Ourselves to Death? How Pessimism, Paranoia, and a Misguided Media Are Leading Us toward Disaster, by H. Aaron Cohl

The Art of Awareness: How Observation Can Transform Your Teaching, second edition, by Deb Curtis and Margie Carter

Arts with the Brain in Mind, by Eric Jensen

At a Loss for Words: How America Is Failing Our Children and What We Can Do about It, by Betty Bardige

Babies in the Rain: Promoting Play, Exploration, and Discovery with Infants and Toddlers, by Jeff A. Johnson

Beyond Behavior Management: The Six Life Skills Children Need, second edition, by Jenna Bilmes

Brain-Based Early Learning Activities: Connecting Theory and Practice, by Nikki Darling-Kuria

Brain-Based Learning: The New Paradigm of Teaching, second edition, by Eric Jensen

Brain Rules: 12 Principles for Surviving and Thriving at Work, Home, and School, by John Medina

Brain Rules for Baby: How to Raise a Smart and Happy Child from Zero to Five, by John Medina

The Brain That Changes Itself: Stories of Personal Triumph from the Frontiers of Brain Science, by Norman Doidge

The Case for Make Believe: Saving Play in a Commercialized World, by Susan Linn

The Case for Mixed-Age Grouping in Early Education, by Lilian G. Katz, Demetra Evangelou, and Jeanette Allison Hartman

Childhood in World History, second edition, by Peter N. Stearns

Consuming Kids: The Hostile Takeover of Childhood, by Susan Linn

Creative Experiences for Young Children, third edition, by Mimi Brodsky Chenfeld

Creativity: Flow and the Psychology of Discovery and Invention, by Mihaly Csikszentmihalyi

Dear Parent: Caring for Infants with Respect, second edition, by Magda Gerber and Joan Weaver

Democracy and Education, by John Dewey

Do-It-Yourself Early Learning: Easy and Fun Activities and Toys from Everyday Home Center Materials, by Jeff A. Johnson and Tasha A. Johnson

Drive: The Surprising Truth about What Motivates Us, by Daniel H. Pink

Einstein Never Used Flash Cards: How Our Children Really Learn—and Why They Need to Play More and Memorize Less, by Kathy Hirsh-Pasek and Roberta Michnick Golinkoff

The Element: How Finding Your Passion Changes Everything, by Ken Robinson, with Lou Aronica

Emergent Curriculum in Early Childhood Settings: From Theory to Practice, by Susan Stacey

Emergent Literacy and Dramatic Play in Early Education, by Jane Davidson

Even More Fizzle, Bubble, Pop & WOW! Simple Science Experiments for Young Children, by Lisa Murphy

Everyday Early Learning: Easy and Fun Activities and Toys Made from Stuff You Can Find around the House, by Jeff A. Johnson, with Zoë Johnson

The Evolving Self: A Psychology for the Third Millennium, by Mihaly Csikszentmihalyi

Finding Flow: The Psychology of Engagement with Everyday Life, by Mihaly Csikszentmihalyi

Finding Your Smile Again: A Child Care Professional's Guide to Reducing Stress and Avoiding Burnout, by Jeff A. Johnson

Five Minds for the Future, by Howard Gardner

Flow: The Psychology of Optimal Experience, by Mihaly Csikszentmihalyi

Fostering Children's Social Competence: The Teacher's Role, by Lilian G. Katz and Diane E. McClellan

Free-Range Kids: Giving Our Children the Freedom We Had without Going Nuts with Worry, by Lenore Skenazy

Get Over It! Relearning Guidance Practices by Daniel J. Hodgins

How Children Fail, by John Holt

How Children Learn, by John Holt

How Children Play, by Ingeborg Haller

How Children Succeed: Grit, Curiosity, and the Hidden Power of Character, by Paul Tough

Huck's Raft: A History of American Childhood, by Steven Mintz

The Hurried Child: Growing Up Too Fast Too Soon, by David Elkind

Infant/Toddler Caregiving: A Guide to Setting Up Environments, by J. Ronald Lally and Jay Stewart

Infant/Toddler Caregiving: A Guide to Social-Emotional Growth and Socialization, by California Department of Education; edited by J. Ronald Lally

Keeping Your Smile: Caring for Children with Joy, Love, and Intention, by Jeff A. Johnson

Keys to Solution in Brief Therapy, by Steve de Shazer

Last Child in the Woods: Saving Our Children from Nature-Deficit Disorder, by Richard Louv

Learning All the Time, by John Holt

Let Them Play: An Early Learning (Un)Curriculum, by Jeff A. Johnson and Denita Dinger

Let's Play: (Un)Curriculum Early Learning Adventures, by Jeff A. Johnson and Denita Dinger

Linchpin: Are You Indispensable?, by Seth Godin

A Mandate for Playful Learning in Preschool: Presenting the Evidence, by Kathy Hirsh-Pasek, Roberta Michnick Golinkoff, Laura E. Berk, and Dorothy G. Singer

Miseducation: Preschoolers at Risk, by David Elkind

The Montessori Method, by Maria Montessori

More Than Miracles: The State of the Art of Solution-Focused Brief Therapy, by Steve de Shazer and Yvonne Dolan

The Myth of the First Three Years: A New Understanding of Early Brain Development and Lifelong Learning, by John T. Bruer

A Nation of Wimps: The High Cost of Invasive Parenting, by Hara Estroff Marano

NurtureShock: New Thinking about Children, by Po Bronson and Ashley Merryman

The Ooey Gooey Handbook, by Lisa Murphy

Out of Our Minds: Learning to be Creative, by Ken Robinson

Parent Power!, by John Rosemond

Play: How It Shapes the Brain, Opens the Imagination, and Invigorates the Soul, by Stuart Brown, with Christopher Vaughan

Play = Learning: How Play Motivates and Enhances Children's Cognitive and Social-Emotional Growth, edited by Dorothy G. Singer, Roberta Michnick Golinkoff, and Kathy Hirsh-Pasek

Play: The Foundation That Supports the House of Higher Learning, by Lisa Murphy

Play: The Pathway from Theory to Practice, by Sandra Heidemann and Deborah Hewitt

Playing to Get Smart, by Elizabeth Jones and Renatta M. Cooper

The Power of Play: Learning What Comes Naturally, by David Elkind

The Quality School Teacher: A Companion Volume to the Quality School, by William Glasser

Ready or Not: Leadership Choices in Early Care and Education, by Stacie G. Goffin and Valora Washington

Right from Birth: Building Your Child's Foundation for Life: Birth to 18 Months, by Craig T. Ramey and Sharon L. Ramey

Secure Relationships: Nurturing Infant/Toddler Attachment in Early Care Settings, by Alice Sterling Honig

Seeking Balance in an Unbalanced World: A Teacher's Journey, by Angela Schmidt Fishbaugh

Swinging Pendulums: Cautionary Tales for Early Childhood Education, by Carol Garhart Mooney